I've been teaching adults for over 30 years.
to" but this book has raised my awareness a
new level. All the teaching skills that I had learned before this book I know
now were the "basics". This is the advanced course!

With this book, I am learning to create the space for myself and my
students to open up to learning, growing and experiencing new ideas at a new
level, the "heart" level. It's magic! I challenge you to read one page -- you
will be compelled to ready the entire book and then re-read again and again.
Your teaching skills will be transformed and you will also be transformed!
Give yourself and your students the gift of the lessons in this book....

Susie Sherry, Associate Faculty. MiraCosta College

Alice Bandy is an amazing master teacher who holds her adult students
enthralled. I found Alice's book *The Heart of Adult Learning* invaluable. This
book is a lesson of how to set the stage for learning to captivate and hold the
adult student's interest. It is a "must have" for anyone interested in working
with students on this level.

Gail Manishor, RScP,

Author of *From Here to Serenity, A Spiritual Guide to Transform Your Life*

Alice Bandy is an excellent teacher, healer and spiritual guide to joyous
living. I love Alice Bandy and I know you will too.

#1 New York Times bestselling author, Debbie Ford

This is a must-read book for anyone who wants to be a heart-centered teacher. Rich and jam-packed with wisdom, storytelling, and inspiration. You will read it more than once. Thank you, Alice Bandy, for being the best guide and teacher for happier living.

Kathy Nelson, CPPC, RScP, owner, On Track Success Coaching

I recently facilitated a group of adults in a nine-week book study. To stimulate learning, I used many of the exercises from *The Heart of Adult Learning*. I began each meeting with a ritual that brought the attention of the group into focus. I created several fun, humorous, and engaging games, as an interactive way to learn the material. I shared poetry that was relevant and heart-opening, as well as meditation and visualization, to bring deeper awareness and openings for wisdom to flow through the students. Finally, I used a creative art project, set to music, at the last class to focus on the beauty and depth of all that we had experienced in nine weeks.

All of these tools and many more thought-provoking ideas from *The Heart of Adult Learning* greatly enhanced the richness of this teaching experience. It was an invaluable aid in creating an atmosphere where adults could have a fun, heart-opening and wisdom-filled experience, not often found in traditional adult learning environments. Thank you, Dr. Alice, for sharing your knowledge and expertise in education, so that all of us can continue to grow, learn and teach adults of any age with confidence.

Carolyn Holder, RScP

The Heart of
Adult
Learning

Ideas, Exercises and Tools
for Helping Your Students Grow

Dr. Alice Bandy

Silver Tree

Published by SilverTree Press, a division of The Heart of Teaching, Inc. A non-profit corporation.
For information address: SilverTree Press, 2240 Encinitas Blvd. Suite D548, Encinitas, CA 92024
www.silvertreepress.com

ISBN 978-0692313053

Cover Design by Trevor Thomas, LightWerxMedia.com

*For all good teachers everywhere
who are making a difference every day.*

For all of my teachers who opened my eyes.

*Especially for my family who opened my heart:
Riley, Elizabeth, Michael, Gene and Barry.
I love you all so much.*

With Gratitude

Producing this book was no small thing. and could not have happened without the inspiration and support of many people. Here are those to whom I am most grateful. With profound thanks to:

Michael Berger, my Editor and partner, whose careful critique and additions to this book made it what it is now. It's an amazing experience to have someone I love walk through every word on every page to help me think deeper and explain myself more clearly. Thank you.

My teachers who lit the way for all that I am and hope to be as a teacher. My dear friend and teacher, Dr. Linda McNamar who is one of the greats. Dr. Chriss Lemmon who taught me more by not explaining than I thought I would ever know. Dr. Dean Brown who opened his heart to me that I might learn everything. The great teachers from across the ages, from Hermes to Socrates, to Thomas Troward, to Joel Goldsmith to all of my friends who are out there teaching and inspiring others today. Especially Parker Palmer, who inspires me every day. Thank you.

For those who lent their expertise to make this book better: Trevor Thomas, whose brilliance and intuition brought beauty to the cover design. Lael Jackson, who stepped in at the final hour, to bring her keen eye and excellent skill with words to the manuscript. Thank you.

My dear friends in the Tree of Life Community. Our adventure is thrilling, and I am so inspired by your love, consciousness, and service to the world. Thank you.

Katherine Economou, my partner in teaching and in fun. Thanks for the hours we steal to renew our hearts and brains, so I can return refreshed to my desk.

All my students everywhere. With every word I write, I am thinking of you. Thank you for your willingness to learn and grow. Because of you, teaching is not only fun, but the love of my life.

Introduction

When I think back over my early education, I can only remember the homework, the rules, the lectures and, occasionally, one bright teacher who made a difference. This continued into college. As I matured, it was fun to notice that some of the professors had a passion for their subject, but it hardly ever touched my life at all.

As a full time general manager, a dozen years later, I returned to school to study for an MBA, and my attitude changed. I was enrolled at Pepperdine University, in a great program for middle managers that allowed me to work during the week, and take classes on the weekend. To begin, we were required to attend a full weekend, out-of-town class to study Human Relations. This involved sitting in a room all weekend with 30 others and no curriculum. To my complete surprise, the professor sat in the back and took notes of what we did. There was no agenda, and no rules other than we could only speak about what was happening in the room. Wow! This weekend was fascinating, emotional, educational, exhausting, rejuvenating, and I learned more in three days than I have learned anywhere since about how to relate to and manage people. By the end of three days, we had made fast friendships, formed working teams, designed goals for our studies, eliminated a few who could not bear the process, and arrived at a deeper understanding of ourselves.

This was my first experience of the work of the famed Carl Rogers and the idea of the empowered student. Like a great teacher can, he opened the door to my passion for experiential learning. This type of education is not only interesting, it is thrilling in its results. And it is this way of education that I have devoted my life to learning and teaching.

It was several more years after completing my degree, while teaching in a graduate program for another university, that I discovered the Secret at the Center of the class. The students were fully employed I.T. managers who had returned to school to get their MBA on weekends. The class topic was strategic planning, and called for me to guide them, step-by-step and week-by-week, through the process. By the end of term, they were to produce a final plan.

While prepping for class, I had an idea. What would happen, I wondered, if I supposed that these students already knew how to do this work when they arrived? What would happen if I trusted in their native intelligence to already have all the answers on this subject? I put the university curriculum aside.

On the first Saturday, I divided the group into teams and gave them the assignment to create a strategic plan for one of their own businesses, which they could choose from the members of their team. All their books and materials could be used. Excitement rose in the room. They began working hard and by the end of the day, each team had produced a plan. As we critiqued these plans in the class, there were questions, of course. But the answers, I found, were already there. If we waited, the answers would emerge from the class itself.

Because of this fast start, this particular class was able to do more in this course than any other. Rather than spend my time teaching, I spent it coaching. We all learned and we all experienced the wisdom at the center of the class in a powerful, life-transforming way.

Since then, I have taught many classes, on many topics, to support adult students in personal growth and transformation. The native genius within each of us, and the higher wisdom we tap into at the center, makes adult classes exciting. As we open our hearts to our students, and as they learn to know that they know, the results of our work are far-reaching. Lives are changed, maybe even the world .

This book holds over twenty years of ideas, tools, and methods I have learned about the heart of adult learning. I offer it to you with love. I hope it serves you well in your important work of teaching adults.

Contents

Learn your theories as well as you can,
but put them aside
when you touch the miracle of a living soul.

CARL JUNG

I. Setting the Intention

THE HIGHEST IDEA OF YOUR CLASS

Ira had a big laugh and a big personality. When he was my student, classes were rollicking and lively: discussions where everyone was involved and stimulated to think bigger. The class was so engaged that they often did not want to take breaks and more than once we stayed late into the evening, following some new train of thought.

Education is not the filling of a pail, but the lighting of a fire.

W.B.YEATS

I often think of Ira when I begin to plan a new course. You might think he was an unusual student, and in many ways, he was. He moved to California from Washington, D.C., where he was a legislative lawyer. Finished with the rat race of politics, he retired young, found a beach front home, and began to take night classes. There was not much about the world that you could teach Ira because he had traveled so far and seen so much. But he had a thirst to grow and understand himself and the great principles of life. He came to me in a philosophy class I was teaching, with his keen mind, questioning skills and robust sense of humor. He was smart as a whip and called forth from me my greatest authenticity. The curriculum opened itself to me in a new way, and together we explored new ways of seeing and bringing life to ancient philosophy.

He was an unusual student with vast experience and a dynamic way of thinking. But he was also very much the same as the students

1

We should take care not to make the intellect our God. It has, of course, powerful muscles, but no personality.

ALBERT
EINSTEIN

you will meet in your classroom when you are teaching adults.

Like Ira, your students bring much to the table. They have lived a lot of their lives already. They have opinions, experiences, and ways of thinking that are uniquely theirs. Like Ira, many of them have not gone back to school for many years, and they have no intention of repeating boring, tedious, rule-based learning that many lived through as children. They have no intention of wasting their time. If your class is not relevant, they will not attend. They are choosing carefully which classes and experiences are worth giving up their weekends or evenings.

No matter how much you love your subject matter, you will not succeed if you do not first consider the expectations of your student. But there is something else that goes deeper. You have an unwritten agreement with these students to assist them in growing. Perhaps it is growing in their careers, or their skills. Perhaps it is growing in their thinking and ways of processing life. But personal growth is the underlying motivator for every adult who returns to class.

That is why it is so important for you to create experiences for your students where they can grow. Your call to teach expands into something quite profound. Not only are you teaching them a skill or passing information, but you are also helping them to lead better lives, They are gathering confidence, new identities, new ways of living and seeing the world. They are taking another shot at being happy with who they are. And you, the teacher, have the wonder of creating the space for this to happen. Your own heart is opening the door for these strangers to come together in mutual respect to support each other in living authentic lives. This is the highest idea of your class, and it is where we begin.

SETTING THE INTENTION

As you begin to set an intention for the class, your ideas must be grounded in love. Love for the individuals in the class and love for the path they are walking are essential. You do not have the power, nor should you try, to "fix" your students, remedy their ills or solve their problems. Nor should you take them on as personal projects. Their wisdom has brought them to class, and their wisdom will guide them into their greater understanding. Your role is to create a space where their process can occur. You must be clear about the material you are teaching, and be sure that you are ready and have the resources necessary to make your class a powerful experience for all.

Nine tenths of education is encourage-ment

ANATOLE FRANCE

It is important to consider the expectations already held for this class. You are the instructor/facilitator, so you have the greatest impact on the intention. But there are other intentions to consider. There is the intention of the author of the material you will be covering, the intention of the place where your class will be held, the intention of the students who will be attending the class, and most importantly, the highest possible intention for this class.

QUESTIONS TO GUIDE YOUR INTENTION

Answering these questions will guide you in setting your intention for your class. Take a couple of deep breaths and allow yourself to welcome whatever answers come. Allow your heart to open and love the process you are beginning with this new class. Trust your inner knowing, your inner teacher.

1. What is the grand idea of this class? What is the highest outcome possible?
2. Why is it important that I am the one to teach this class?
3. What personal growth or understanding will I receive because of this class?
4. Why are these students attending? What is the highest benefit to them?
5. What must I do to embrace fully the greatest intentions for this class?

Review your answers to these questions and begin to write out your intention. Be sure to include yourself and your personal intentions.

Sample intentions:

My intention is to use the works of Emerson as a catalyst for each student to remember their originality and independent spirit. My intention for myself is to remain open to any inspiration I can share about how to live more courageously in the world, as Emerson did.

My intention is to use the experience and principles of Group Dynamics as a mirror for each student to better understand themselves and how to work with others. My intention for myself is to trust the group and to learn by witnessing the students growing in their abilities through our class in Group Dynamics.

WHAT WILL YOU TEACH?

There are infinite ideas for subjects to teach. You may choose to lead a class based upon a book you love, an idea that moves you, or you a set curriculum provided for you. It is important to review your material and make a list of the ideas that seem most important to you. Use this list to organize your class week by week. Be sure that you are emphasizing each week an idea that moves you personally.

Remember that it is no accident that you are the one leading this class. Your unique talents, interests, sense of humor, spiritual understanding, experiences - all of who you are is brought to this class on purpose. Your students signed up for this class, at some level, because you are the teacher. So trust yourself and your instincts. Teach who you are. Teach what you love. Share your inner journey with your students. It is said that students will drive a thousand miles to be in the presence of one who has had an individual experience of truth. Share your personal experiences.

WHAT WILL YOU LEARN?

The corollary of your being the chosen teacher is that you are also the chosen learner. We are all teachers, and we are all learners. When you learn a new idea, discover a new practice, achieve some mastery of spiritual principles, you naturally share it with someone else. We find in the classroom that the minute the light goes on for one person, they share it with another student. This dynamic is integral to life and the path we are walking. We are all teachers; we are all learners. This ripple effect continues through time and space for all of us.

This exciting idea reveals the richness and importance of community. One who sits at home cannot discover these rich experiences of mutual learning and mutual teaching. Loners have to do both for themselves. Community is an important reason that people are called to attend your class. They do not come just to learn from you. They also come to teach you and to learn from others. This exchange is a great gift of our human experience. We all thrive and grow more powerfully together than we could ever do on our own.

Before I can tell my life what I want to do with it, I must listen to my life telling me who I am.

PARKER PALMER

LIFE IS A TEXTBOOK

Life is a textbook for your class. No matter how great the readings or how clever your handouts are, life has its way with the class. Each person brings to their study a set of experiences that are wonderfully unique. Each has a family or set of friends that are crisscrossing across their daily schedules. Each has emotions, dreams and ways of thinking. As the conversations and discussions begin in class, you can listen and hear the voice of their lives being expressed. As a teacher, it is up to you to support them.

For example, if one of your students has a hard week and starts to share their challenges in class, everyone benefits. Everyone finds in that story a reflection of their own story in some way. Everyone begins to sort within their inner resources to see what they would do or did under similar circumstances. For some, another's issue may trigger their desire to teach, and they may want to offer advice. Advising is not OK in personal group sharing. If someone is not free to share their experience without another student solving it for them, they will stop sharing. You as the instructor can support the student in their sharing. But it is never correct for you or any other student to solve the problem for them. Trust that they are capable and can find their own answers.

We are honoring the personal life of the student, not matching wits to see who can be right or who knows more. We are asking the shy soul to speak into the group and by revealing itself, to find its voice. This is not the case in regular class work discussions when you want to encourage an active give and take amongst students. Rather, I mean those times when a student offers a personal experience of their life.

So, when other students want to take this opportunity to teach other students how to live, it is important to remind them that this is not not the place.

Mentors and apprentices are partners in an ancient human dance,
and one of teaching's great rewards is the daily chance it gives us to
get back on the dance floor. It is the dance of the spiraling
generations, in which the old empower the young with their
experience and the young empower the old with new life, reweaving
the fabric of the human community as they touch and turn.

PARKER PALMER

When an individual has the courage to speak personal questions into the class, he/she finds a powerful way of communicating in life.

We will be discussing how to create a sacred space for sharing in Chapter Five. The point I want to make here is that everyone's life can serve as the curriculum for everyone else. It is up to you to take advantage of someone's example to teach better ways of thinking and living. Let life be the curriculum for your classroom.

WHERE DOES YOUR GREAT GLADNESS MEET THE WORLD'S NEED?

This question is asked by Frederick Buechner, one of the great writers of our time. It encapsulates the important final criteria for setting an intention for your class. I love it because it is based upon one of the essential truths of life. We cannot suppress our passions and have personal growth. We must be authentic with ourselves and with each other.

As the teacher of this class, your must ask yourself this question: Where does my great gladness meet the world's need? If creativity makes you glad, then it must be the intention of your class to express that creativity. Your enthusiasm will inspire all who attend.

If music fills your heart, then your classes must be filled with music. Those who love it will be attracted to your class.

If you love to move and hike and be out of doors, then your classes must do this also. So many love nature and your great gladness will speak to them too.

If you love intellectual sparring and a lively discussion, your class must include a dynamic give and take of ideas. When you express your great gladness, the world will find you.

There are two kinds of teachers: the kind that fill you with so much quail shot that you can't move, and the kind that gives you a little prod behind and you jump into the skies.

ROBERT FROST

7

CREATING THE CLASS IN CONSCIOUSNESS

One of the great thinkers of the19th century, Thomas Troward, advanced the idea of creating a spiritual prototype of the experiences we want in our lives. This idea is based upon the ancient wisdom that all of our life experience first begins within.

You are essentially beginning to work with the energy of the class as you plan it, set your intention, and create the materials. Your passion and excitement start to build, and the inner prototype of this class begins to form. It's as if your heart and mind hold an inner blueprint for how the class will go. As your pattern becomes stronger and more real, it starts to play out in the actual class.

Here are a few ideas for how to harness the power of creating your class in consciousness before it begins.

1. INVITING THEM IN
Spend time with the idea that you have set the intention, and now you are inviting students to join the class. Sit down, close your eyes and imagine your students before you. Open your mind and invite them in. Open your heart with love to all of those who will be part of this class.

2. CREATING THE SPACE
At least a month in advance, use your imagination to create the space in which you will be holding your class. In our busy world, available rooms are usually serving many purposes. Whether in a classroom, a community center, or your living room, claim this space as the place in time in which your class will be held.

Sit quietly and picture the room in your mind. We are only claiming this space for the exact hours of your class, not for all times. So be intentional in imagining this room at 6 p.m. on your class night, or whatever time it will be. Imagine that this space is a powerful place filled up with the energy of your class. I like to imagine colors for this energy since it makes it more real. Choose a favorite color, but stay away from black, brown, white and grey.

Imagine that there is a bubble of this color hanging in the air in the middle of the room. As you watch, imagine that this bubble begins to expand until it fills the entire room, touching all four walls, the ceiling and the floor. Let this bubble become so real to you that you do not have to put any extra energy into the room. Once this process is complete, you can just step out of it and not think too much about it. Check back every week or so to see that it is still in place.

I have had many experiences of having no registrations for class and then having it suddenly fill up once I have set the color for the room. I have also taught this to very inexperienced teachers and watched them attract large crowds to their classes the first time out. So try it before you decide it doesn't work.

YOUR TRANSPARENT HEART

Now that you have invited your students in and created a space in consciousness for your class to take place, it is important to surrender to the process of being yourself. Your unique passions, loves, experiences, perspectives all make up what you are - a teacher for this class.

Spend time in preparing yourself. Take the grand vision for what is possible in this new teaching experience. Dream of all the good that will come from it. You are the window through which the light of this new learning experience flows into the classroom. Be glad! Let your heart be transparent and clear about your intentions, your willingness to teach and your availability to learn. Place yourself in service to the support of those who are brave and open enough to come to class. And so your next adventure in teaching begins.

Our deepest calling is to grow into our own authentic self-hood. whether or not it conforms to some image of who we ought to be. As we do so, we will not only find the joy that every human being seeks--we will also find our path of authentic service in the world.

PARKER PALMER

2. Making Your Class Work

BEING PREPARED

When coming home from a conference recently, I arrived at the Monterey airport to find long lines of travelers waiting for departures. A cloud bank was sitting on the Monterey peninsula, not unusual for the early morning, and we were all waiting for it to clear for takeoff. At that same moment, a friend called my cell to offer a ride home in her car.

The man who can make hard things easy is the educator.

EMERSON

I had a decision to make: wait for the weather to clear for a 2-hour plane ride or take the offer of a 6-hour drive. Intuitively, I took the offer of a ride. I was home having a nice dinner while the air travelers got stuck overnight and could not get back.

It's a little hard to describe how we all make these kinds of decisions every day: which road to take, which store to shop, which appointment to set. In the same vein, students often say to me: "I just felt that I should sign up for the class." Or, alternatively, they may say, "It just didn't seem to be the right time to take it." The name of the class usually does not convey to the student what the value of the class will be to them. How you create the course does.

So, if you have ever heard these same words from students, or wondered why your class attendance is low, I will give you the answer: *Preparation*. We are highly intuitive, complex beings and at

The secret in education lies in respecting the student.

EMERSON

some subliminal level we know what will be enjoyable for us and what will not. Adult students, who have many choices for how to spend their time, are highly sensitive to which classes will benefit them, even if they cannot explain it. Many times, I have had very little response to a class I am offering until I prepare it. Once I prepare, the registration fills up. As it becomes more real for me, it becomes more real for the student. And it begins to take form.

To begin your preparation for class, there are some basic areas of the class experience to address. Here are questions to ask when preparing your class:

HOW WILL YOU CREATE A SAFE SPACE?

The great educator is one who can create a space where each person feels safe to share their journey and their ideas: to take the risk of learning, changing, and growing without fear of ridicule, criticism, or advice. Why no advice? This is an important point. Advice adds ideas to the conversation but does not empower your student. To lead successful lives, they must find these answers for themselves. It is important that you see through your students' outer appearance to the accomplished individuals that they are.

Adults bring with them life experiences and insights that will add greatly to your class. They have already found their way and have, to some degree, an understanding of themselves. Every survey and statistic shows that adult students want to be respected, valued and heard. And yet, as teachers we want our students to continue to grow and learn, even in their maturity. Our job is to assist them in being able to express themselves, share their ideas, ask their questions, and make a true contribution to the class.

If your class is well prepared and effective, your adult student can find solutions for themselves. Encourage them to listen to the guidance of their own hearts. Empower them to know that they can learn, change, and make good choices for themselves. Teach this idea to all your students so that your classroom becomes a safe place to learn and grow.

There is such a gift in simply being heard. Offer the opportunity to be heard, without judgment. Being heard creates a softening of resistance and a greater willingness to participate. This alone is a great assistance for many people because, by being heard, they recover faith in themselves. It is important to explain this to your group and to let them know that there will be no advising or fixing of each other's problems during discussions.

Which brings up the next point: all members of your class must agree that what is shared personally in the class is confidential. It is not secret but is it sacred. Their agreement to this idea makes your class a safe space for all. Each person is free to share their own experience of the class with their family and friends. But they are not free to share anyone else's experience or the details of anyone else's life. In this way, your class forms a sense of community and support that can make it an effective, and transformative learning experience.

Elements of Every Class

- Greeting of each student
- Opening of class with an inspiring idea or ritual
- Opportunity for each student to speak into the room, either through introduction, or other personal sharing. It helps to bond the group and build community.
- Introduction to this week's class, either through introduction of a new topic, summary of last session, relevant story, or other.
- Class discussion of material and ideas for the week
- Questions and answers
- Break for socializing, community building and change of class energy
- Experiential Exercise to have an experience of the material
- Time for the group to share their thoughts about the exercise and material
- Closing of class

HOW WILL YOU CREATE A BEAUTIFUL SPACE?

*What
sculpture
is to a
block of
marble,
education
is to the
soul.*

JOSEPH
ADDISON

Let's think about beauty for a moment. What is beautiful to you? Do you love to see the moonlight on a summer's night? Do you love the soft touch of a child's hand in yours? Are your inner feelings stirred by the sound of a beautiful piece of music? Does your eye delight in the colors of a field of flowers? Does your mind come to rest when walking down a shady lane of deeply green trees? If you can remember these sensations, you are close to understanding how to stimulate and empower your class through beauty in the classroom.

Remember, students will be spending hours together in this classroom. As educators, we want to invoke the highest gifts and talents of the full person. We want to harness the power of the mind, the intuition of the heart, and the genius of the spirit of each student, so that each learns, grows, and develops through this class.

So, let's begin by considering the space in which you will be teaching your class. If you are fortunate, perhaps it will be held in a space that has already been cared for and loved. This is usually not the case. We often find that classes are held in a place that is functional but not beautiful. Probably, it is used by others for other things. It is up to you to make it sacred, beautiful and stimulating.

Begin by standing back and looking at it. Your senses will guide you in creating the class space. What do you see? Is it attractive or is it cluttered or messy. If so, it must be straightened up, and cleared.

Are there phone cords, extension cords, staplers, and other unattractive items lying around? All extra cords must be unplugged or hidden and office items put away. Are there computers or other technology in the rooms that give it a work-related feel? If so, consider draping colorful scarves over them or moving them where they are not a strong influence in the room.

What is the lighting situation? Are there glaring overhead lights? Is there any natural light? When possible, use indirect rather than overhead light to create a softer ambiance. If natural light is available, open the curtains or blinds and let it into the room.

Is there activity visible from some adjoining room or hallway? If so, close the door or place a plant in the way, to act as a screen. Is there a clock? The student may like the clock, but the heart is timeless. Remove the clock if possible.

Your eye will guide you in transforming this space. Once you have straightened the room as much as possible with what is already there, consider what you can add to the room to make it beautiful.

Flowers are, I believe, an essential element for self-development classwork. They can be artificial or real, but they must be lovely to look at and, preferably, placed around the room where the eye can fall upon them during the class. Green plants are also very good for this purpose. Inexpensive artificial ones will do the job if live plants are not available.

Consider art for the room. Can you hang a nice print or bring in a real piece of art for the room? Ideally everywhere you look in the classroom will have some point of beauty. This is lovely for the eye

It is only with the heart that one can see rightly; what is essential is invisible to the eye.

ANTOINE de SAINT-EXUPERY

Like a wild animal, the soul is tough, resilient, resourceful, savvy and self-sufficient: it knows how to survive in hard places. Yet despite its toughness, the soul is also shy. Just like a wild animal, it seeks safety in the dense underbrush, especially when other people are around. If we want to see a wild animal, we know that the last thing we should do is go crashing through the woods and yelling for it to come out. But if we will walk quietly into the woods, sit patiently at the base of a tree, breathe with the earth, and fade into our surroundings, the wild creature we seek might put in an appearance.

PARKER PALMER, *To Know As We Are Known*

and sets the stage for the heart to soften and the student to feel safe in expressing themselves there.

Does this seem like a lot of work? Try it and see how it makes a difference to your students. When you take the time to honor their deep love of beauty and create a sacred space to enter, your class grows in power and everyone benefits.

Is the room quiet? If so, you may choose to either leave it that way or to add some nice music. I have found, particularly with beginning classes, that music is a great assistance in creating class space and putting the students at ease. When you arrive for class, put on soft music, just loud enough to fill the room. The students usually come in full of chatter and greeting for each other, and they cannot hear the music through the commotion and noise. However, as they begin to get settled in their chairs, they notice the music and begin to become more quiet. As you begin the class, turn the music down even more so it is soft and a nice background for your opening remarks. Turn it off during class itself.

One final note on sound. If this room has traffic noise, people noise,

A Classroom Blessing

Sit quietly at the head of the room. Notice the beauty of the space you have created. Notice the 4 corners of the space or the outer boundaries of this space and see them each grounded into the earth with a river of gold light. Acknowledge the blessings already in place for this class:

> *the power of the north to inspire courage and leadership*
> *the power of the east to inspire new beginnings*
> *the power of the south to inspire love and an honoring of life*
> *the power of the west to inspire creativity and expression*

Acknowledge the power of this group of people coming together, already having so much wisdom and insight and understanding. See light shining at the center of the room and growing, shining into every nook and cranny, touching the walls, filling the room with light. Acknowledge the love that has called this class together. Feel this love permeating this room. This is a space of love that is safe for all who enter here. And so, be grateful. Say a prayer of gratitude for this room, for all who enter it, and for all that takes place here. All of it is a blessing.

construction, or other noise from the outside, you must address it before the class begins. Try closing the windows, finding out about construction hours and asking for a change, asking others to be more quiet. If these do not work, then you will need to plan for an activity, conversation, and more noise in your classroom during the noisy period.

Wherever you are, be there.

EMERSON

How does the room feel? How does it smell? This is very personal, but use your reactions as the guideline for creating the feeling in the room. Does it smell musty or dusty or have another odor? If so, the odor must be removed, and the room cleaned up. This idea extends to the restroom facilities and entrance way. All must be clean, and clutter free with a nice odor or no odor at all. I recently taught at a lovely facility, but it had wilting flowers and cobwebs all around the entrance. I spent an hour with a hose, watering the flowers and washing down the front door, eaves and side walls to the entrance. Give yourself some time to check this all out and take care of it before the first class meeting.

REGARDING QUESTIONS OF TIME

I encourage you to consider your personal attitude about time. Many Americans and those from a few other countries have a fondness for promptness while other countries are more casual about time. As the teacher of the class, you get to decide how the class will regard time.

I am mentioning this because many teachers feel automatically that every class must start and stop on time. The human heart has no real interest in time. Most adults lead busy, stressful lives, juggling family, jobs, relationships, other commitments. The last thing you want is for your class to add to the stress in their lives.

About altars

There is a great interest in altars today and not only for religious purposes. Altars in the purest sense are an outward picture of an inward journey. By arranging physical objects of significance in a place of honor, we begin to symbolize the meaning of our experience together. We have many examples of this kind of thing: red roses at Valentine's Day to symbolize love. Wonderful white flowers for a funeral to symbolize love and honor of the spirit who has departed. Eggs to symbolize the renewal of life in the spring at Easter. And many more. An altar in your classroom can use symbolism to bring added importance to your time together.

You may wish to consider the use of an altar to symbolize the content and purpose of your class. If you are teaching a class on parenting, you might ask students to bring pictures of their children and provide items that represent them as parents. If you are teaching a class on geography, you might include a globe and pictures from other countries grouped together.

Asking everyone to participate in the creation of the altar, creates a sense of community and an outward representation of the class process. This can be very powerful for the group. Ask each student to bring something from home to symbolize their intentions in the class.

The altar can sit in the middle of the class table, on a small bookcase or table to the side of the group, or at the very center of the room. Consider what sorts of colors, objects, flowers, candles, symbols, statues, etc. would be appropriate for your subject matter.

When holding classes on subjects that affect our human lives, such as relationship, prosperity or health, I try to use nature symbols: branches, leaves, flowers, stones, water, fire. When holding classes on more spiritual topics, such as philosophy, grief, or ethics, I use only a lovely vining plant and a single white candle, to symbolize the oneness of life. You can use fun symbols to represent a journey: road maps, toy cars, or planes. You can use sentimental symbols: old pictures, paper hearts, diaries. It is very powerful to invite each of your class members to bring their own candle for the altar. At the close of class, especially at night, light all the candles, dim the lights, and experience a flood of candlelight as a symbol of the power of this class.

Experiment and enjoy the possibilities of an altar in your classroom. If you would like more about altars, I recommend the book Altars by Denise Linn.

For this reason, I encourage you to be relaxed about the start time. As the class members begin to gather, take time to welcome each. Give everyone a chance to get settled and relax a little before the class begins. Just a few minutes of this kind of latitude sets a relaxed tone. When your students feel recognized, welcomed, and relaxed, they can focus better and have a more powerful experience of your class.

Our intention is not to waste anyone's time, especially those who like to start on the minute. All we want is to create a safe, welcoming time when the class can get settled - maybe 5 minutes or so. Can you arrange that no one is embarrassed to arrive a little late? I tell my adult students; it is better to come late than not to come at all. For that reason, I greet each student warmly, no matter what time they arrive. However, if you find most of the class beginning to arrive 10 or 15 minutes late, you will want to tighten it up. One way to do this is to plan something very interesting to happen in class within the first 10 minutes. A few experiences of this and you will see your students starting to arrive on time.

Try as much as possible to end on time. Your students are busy people and have many other responsibilities, babysitters, deadlines, meetings, etc in their lives. If the class runs longer than usual for some reason, be sure to get the group agreement that they are willing to stay an extra 15 minutes or so to finish up. Your students will appreciate being asked and participating in their learning experience.

Education's purpose is to replace an empty mind with an open one.

MALCOLM
FORBES

HOW WILL YOU GREET YOUR STUDENTS?

One of our most important human interactions is the greeting when we first see each other. It is especially important in family, community, or class settings. Adult students are sometimes nervous about returning to school or preoccupied with their personal responsibilities. How we greet them will set the tone for how our relationship unfolds today. It is important to make a point of greeting each student with love and respect.

At the start of some classes, I stand at the door of the class and greet them as they enter. At the very least, I try to greet them before they sit down. Touch is a powerful experience, and shaking their hand is very honoring; giving them a brief hug can be nice, if it is appropriate to your group. You will know immediately if they are resistant to being hugged. Do not insist on this, even if you like it. Strangers are sometimes hesitant to touch, but a warm handshake can set a nice tone for welcoming them to class. It is an unspoken exchange that sets the foundation for how you will relate to each other during the class.

This greeting honors the whole person in front of you. Use the senses. Look directly into their eyes, smile, give a warm greeting. Within the silence of your mind say hello to the heart of this human being before you. Here they are, willing to grow, to risk, and to learn. It is your privilege to serve and to be the one who supports them in change. Begin with a personal, respectful greeting every time.

HOW WILL YOU ENGAGE THE WHOLE PERSON?

There is a beautiful old story told about a small village in the hills of China that was isolated from the outside world. On the other side of the great mountain grew a special herb that brewed the most delicious tea. This tea was wonderful and considered to be a great treasure. And so the village potter created a very beautiful and very special teapot in which only this tea was brewed.

We rarely hear the inward music,
but we are still all dancing to it nevertheless.
RUMI

20

Every fall, before the rains came, the men of the village would climb the great mountain and bring back this special herb. Then the women would place it in a beautiful pot and add the boiling water for just the right amount of time. The entire village would gather and share this delicious tea.

It became a regular festival held each fall. This went on for hundreds of years. Until one year when the rains came early, and there was no time to gather the herb. Everyone was distressed. Then one young woman had an idea and brought out the great pot, poured in the boiling water, waited a few minutes and behold. The flavor was delicious! The pot had brewed the special tea for so many years that it was no longer necessary to have the herb. The pot itself was so steeped in the great flavor that it could create the tea itself.

This simple story reveals so much of the truth of the learning process. We can add facts and data and even spirited discussion about any topic we are teaching. But not until our student has embodied this lesson, will they become one who can take the new ideas into their lives and fully live them.

So, we have a big task in teaching meaningful adult classwork. We must provide all the ingredients for the whole person, our adult student, to embody these ideas, find meaning in them, and transform through them. We must offer enough intellectual material to entertain the mind; enough inspirational matter to open the heart. And enough experiential work to engage the body.

For this reason, be sure each session of your class has something for each aspect of the human being. Plan an inspiring moment of some sort, whether it is a quotation, meditation, contemplation, or ritual. Plan new ideas to engage the mind. Consider reading material, points for group discussion, or a lecture. Plan a moment for socializing, sharing, and connecting with each other. Plan for an experiential exercise to provide an opportunity for practice and embodiment of the lesson. This exercise can be anything that uses the body to give an experience of your subject. There is a knack to creating these kinds of experiential exercises, and we will be discussing this further in Chapter Six.

HOW WILL YOU INVOKE THE HEART?

So much of the power of your class depends upon you and your constant awareness that these students are human beings with wise hearts and spirits. Ask yourself, "How would I speak to the heart of this person? How will I love the stranger before me?" It is profound and subtle work to arrive at this answer. But it is real.

These adult students have returned to class to better their lives. But they are also interested in the eternal verities of life and in becoming a better person. No matter what your subject is, your class can support each of them in growing and changing. Give your students opportunities to be kind and loving, to speak the truth, to be generous, and to have the faith of their convictions.

When we, as teachers, encourage adults to trust their personal choices and to embody the learning of our classes, we are fulfilling our purposes in teaching.
As Galileo said: "*You cannot teach a man anything. You can only help him discover it within himself.*"

RHYTHM OF THE CLASS

There are endless approaches to establishing a rhythm for your class. Like a beautiful piece of music or a dance, the class moves to a hidden rhythm, and you are the one who creates it. Plan it the same as you might for small children. Do not keep them in one place for extended periods of time. Adults do not learn well from being lectured to for hours. Think participation. Make your important points and then put the students into small groups, partners or dyads to discuss the subject or solve a problem. Brainstorm solutions, instead of giving answers. Think about moving vs. sitting, speaking vs. listening, reading vs. doing, silence vs. music, pictures vs. words, sharing vs. journaling. The important idea is to keep changing every 15 to 30 minutes. Changing the pace keeps your class lively, interesting, and relevant.

Here is my rough idea of the rhythm of a 3 hour class. You can use it as a starting point for your class preparation.

PLANNING CLASS FLOW

ACTIVITY	WAY OF LEARNING
Greeting and settling in 5 minutes	social
Opening inspiration, reading, quote, ritual, etc. 10 minutes	hearing, seeing
Questions and answers or sharing from students 20 minutes	participation
Presentation of today's topic/recap of last week 20 minutes	listening/thinking
Discussion 10 minutes	participation
Small group work on the topic 30 minutes	talking. problem solving
Break 15 minutes	social, movement
Summary of where we are and topic elaboration 10 minutes	listening/thinking
Experiential exercise 30 minutes	experience
Sharing of ideas and reactions to the exercise 15 minutes	participation, talking
Discussion of next week 5 minutes	listening/participating
Any final comments question 5 minutes	participation
Close and goodbye 5 minutes	

In this chapter, we have discussed the basics of your work in preparing the class and setting the proper atmosphere and tone. Important questions must be answered and the proper attention planned before class begins. Don't try shortcuts with these ideas. Your day-to-day class will unfold so much more easily and so much more powerfully, when you give thoughtful consideration and careful preparation ahead of time. Once you are complete with all of this work, you are ready to begin.

In the next chapter, we will consider how to open your class session.

RULES OF THUMB

Everything discussed about an individual's life is CONFIDENTIAL We are creating a safe space for all to express, learn, and grow.

Discourage students from giving advice. Teach them to support each other with compassion and have confidence in each to handle their own issues.

Never criticize a student in front of the group. If they are behaving inappropriately, deal with them privately so as not to humiliate them in the group.

Try to honor and protect the scapegoats in the class. They are expressing the hidden fears of the collective group consciousness. Treat them with respect.

Discourage hypothetical questions. Adults are interested in real life experiences, so encourage students to ask real questions that pertain to real issues.

If the group should become unmanageable for any reason, STOP. Take a moment of silence. Let the answers emerge from within the class and yourself.

Discourage long-winded stories. Instead ask students to focus on what insights they gained from this experience that could benefit the class.

During the discussion, give students the opportunity to pass if they do not want to contribute. Participation increases in an atmosphere of freedom and acceptance.

Gently mediate group discussion, pulling the conversation back to the central theme, without presenting yourself as an authority on the subject.

Never assume you have a consensus. Before you move forward, check for consensus. If is necessary to move on without consensus, acknowledge it. Otherwise, students will not trust you. Encourage them to voice their preferences.

Close on time. If you must go over your time, ask the permission of the group. If some students must leave at the designated time, give them permission to go.

3. Openings

GETTING OFF TO A GREAT START

Many mornings I like to hike in the canyon near my home. In the early light, the sky is lovely to behold and the landscape shifts in colors of tan, rose and blue. Walking in the quiet, I reflect upon my life and my own heart, and find answers for the new day that is dawning. Frequently, as I am in the midst of this, another neighbor will come along with her dogs off leash. Her pets are boisterous in their morning freedom - running, playing, and having a grand time.

Treat people as if they were what they ought to be and you help them become what they are capable of being.

GOETHE

Then, they have to consider me, coming upon them on the path. Or rather, we have to consider each other. First, we eye each other, internally settling on our idea of each other. Then we approach, and the animals always want a good sniff of me and. perhaps, a brief pat before continuing. I am friendly, and after a brief, close encounter, we all are comfortable with each other and relaxed. I return to my contemplations, and they continue with their morning run.

I sometimes think of them when I am arriving for class. Our need to take stock of each other, to greet each other, and to find our balance with each other is not so different. It is our animal nature and our human nature that wants to be greeted, to settle and to move into a balance of comfort with each other. And, even more than our greeting, we want to do the same with the class experience. We each

25

Be who
you are
and say
what you
feel.
Those
who mind
don't
matter
and those
who
matter
don't
mind.

DR. SUESS

want to answer the unspoken question: how will we work together today? Moving into the class material, we wonder: will this experience be one where I enjoy learning interesting new things?

Deciding how to open the class each week is one of the most important decisions you will make when planning each session. Your opening sets the tone for each week. Your class will be more dynamic if you vary the way class begins. You can open with a game, with sharing, with a ritual, with silence, with an icebreaker or one of many other approaches. Here are a few ideas to consider when planning your class opening.

A PERSONAL GREETING

A personal greeting from you each week is essential to create the level of communication you intend with your students today. Acknowledging them as a person and as an important participant puts the class on much deeper level. Including touch or a brief hug into this greeting is very powerful. Remember you are doing more than just building rapport with this person. You are opening your heart to your students as a safe space for them during their study.

You are opening up to authentic communication, a heart-to -heart understanding, which is important in working with adults. We have all had enough of shallow, impersonal communication. We all love to feel connected and included.

Decide for yourself the best way to accomplish this personal greeting. Will you stand up and greet each student as they wander in? Will you greet them at the door? Personally, I like to wait until all are seated and settled and then I walk around the room and greet each student. This is the way all of my classes begin.

RITUALS TO BEGIN

Ritual can make a big impact at the class opening. Ritual enacts in outer symbols what is occurring on the inside. So, if you want to create a special atmosphere in the classroom, create a ritual to honor the space. To build community, create a ritual in which each person can share a part of themselves with the group. If you wish to begin a new topic, create a ritual for leaving behind the old ideas and starting anew. To honor the content of the class, create a ritual that creates a place of honor for the wisdom of the class.

It is all easier than it seems. Just ask yourself: what is the symbol of this time together? What is the inner work that is happening? Ritual can be powerful and very effective in setting the tone of your class session. Keep your rituals surprising and do not repeat them every time. If you are uncertain of how to do rituals, there are many good books devoted entirely to the subject.

Experiment and be creative in your ritual ideas. No matter what ritual you choose, I encourage you to make it beautiful, engage all the senses, bring a respectful, sacred attitude to it and work with symbols. Once you try a few, you will get the hang of it and the students will love it as a way to open your class.

Ideas for Opening Rituals

- Have a pitcher of water and linen towel on a table by the door. Ask each person to wash their hands entering the room, and leave behind the worries of the day.
- Place a basket in the center. Ask each to place some personal object out of their pocket or purse into the basket, to symbolize the coming together of the group.
- Offer each student the opportunity to speak into the room, either through introduction, or other personal sharing.
- Ask students to move around the room and greet each other.
- Lead the class in an inner process of welcoming the wisdom of all the great thinkers before them.. Light a candle to represent the presence of this wisdom.

HOT STARTS

If you have knowledge, let others light their candles in it.

MARGARET FULLER

In the business world, a hot start is a way of motivating employees. For example, assignments are left on the employee's desk the night before. When employees arrive in the morning, rather than hanging at the water cooler or returning personal emails, they have tasks in front of them to accomplish. A hot start helps them to focus, be more productive, and get off to a faster start in the morning. It creates a busy, creative energy in the office, right from the beginning.

Translating this idea to the classroom means that you have prepared something for the student to do, and it is on their table or chair when they arrive. Hot starts can be used successfully when the class is very chatty, and you feel that the class usually spends too much time getting started. I have used it to engage students at the start of class and correct habitually late arriving students.

Upon arrival, they sit down and complete the task in front of them. At the scheduled class time, begin to discuss this experience with them. Thus, when the latecomer arrives, the discussion is underway, and they realize the merits of being on time. This is an effective way to encourage promptness and avoids embarrassing the tardy adult student, which is counterproductive.

There are two mistakes one can make along the path to truth: not going all the way and not starting.

THE BUDDHA

IDEAS FOR HOT STARTS

For classes where participants drag in late every week: Create a high energy, entertaining exercise in pairs, trios, or small groups. Relate it directly to the course content. It can be short case studies, tough discussion questions, success stories and why they worked. Here are some ideas:

- A personal questionnaire about experiences or attitudes about class topics. For example, questions about the student's earliest ideas of the topic

- A crossword puzzle based upon terms they are learning in class. Check out the HotPotatoes.com software online for creating these.

- A brief quote from the text and questions about it for the student to answer.

- A game or visual puzzle related to the subject matter

- Creating stories.

- For conservative audiences: create a flip chart that says "horror stories" and another that says "success stories", each with colorful illustrations. Divide the class into pairs, trios, or small groups. Ask each small group to create an amusing success story or horror story related to the class content. It need only be a title and the main story points. When complete, ask each group to share their story with the class.

- Case Studies. Create dyads, triads, or small groups and ask each group to discuss a case study related to the subject matter. Write their answers to the case study on the flip chart. When the groups are finished, play some lively music and ask the groups to circulate and read the other group's answers. During the class, tie these answers into the class discussion.

MIXED BLESSINGS OF QUIET OPENINGS

You were born with wings. Why prefer to crawl through life?

RUMI

It can be mixed blessing to start your class with a moment of silence, a visualization, contemplation, or a meditation. Depending on your style of teaching, you may or may not be comfortable beginning your classes with these tools. On one hand, they set a nice sacred tone and bring the students together in consciousness. On the other hand, meditation can put an evening class to sleep and prove to be dull for students who are not used to this practice. A quiet opening may be nice, but it is important to decide if your group will benefit from it.

If you want to use a quiet start to your class, look for some balance. Use some soft music before you start, to set a relaxed tone. Consider your tired adult learner who is leading a busy life. If you decide to use a quiet opening, follow up with something to energize the class and lift the energy of the group.

In my experience, when the class begins with a quiet start, it can be very warm and heart opening. It can also take a good half hour to bring the energy of the room up to a dynamic learning level. Before you begin, plan for what comes next after a quiet class opening.

GAMES

Games are wonderful teaching tools. Adult learners love them, and they energize the classroom. A great class opener is to create a card game based upon the subject matter of the class. As students arrive, ask them to sit around tables in groups of 5 to 7 and give them the game to play. If you have never done this, it is a lot easier than it sounds. Inexpensive 3x5 index cards available everywhere are perfect for creating card games. You can also use the attractive, already-perforated, card stock intended for printing business cards.

When creating your card game, go back to basics and stick with the rules of Old Maid or Fish. This way, your students can play the game making pairs of cards that hold concepts from the class. It is fun, and students learn while they play.

There are other games to create, of course. Let your creativity be your guide. I have seen very clever versions created of Trivial Pursuit, Jeopardy, Charades, all using ideas from the class material. These and more are fun, high energy ways for a class to begin. They are amazingly effective in familiarizing your class with the basic concepts you are teaching.

What worked yesterday is the gilded cage of tomorrow.

PETER BLOCK

EASY GAMES TO START YOUR CLASS

Card Games
Select a card game such as Rummy, Crazy Eights, or Concentration as an overlay for your game. Prepare your playing cards, each card holding content that is relevant to the course. When the class is ready to begin, put on some lively music and give each group of 2 to 5 students a deck of your cards. Pass out brightly colored sheets of instructions. Allow the game to continue until everyone has arrived, or the game is complete. Give prizes to the winners.

Word Search Puzzles
Prepare questions that are relevant to the course material and a word search puzzle that contains the answers. Ask the students to partner up and use the puzzle to find the answers to the questions. Play some lively music. Give prizes to the winners. Check out HotPotato.com software for making these puzzles.

Mixer Game
Create a series of questions about the course content and write one question each on index cards. Also create the answers to the questions and write one answer each on an index card. Ask student to take one from each deck. They then walk around and ask their question and find the person who has the answer to their question. If they find it, they can pull another question. The one who finds the most answers to the most questions wins! Give a prize.

Example: ADULT LEARNING GAME

Here is a game I designed for a class of teachers to teach them the basic principles of adult learning. Use this game format to teach a list of new ideas.

Preparation:

Prepare a deck of 50 cards for playing. On each 3x5 card, write a short one or two-word concept that is true about adult learning. Make a pair for it, so there are two of each kind of card. For example, I made two cards that say: "Class Favorite: Open Discussion." Two more that say: "Class favorite: Experiential learning." And so on, until there are 25 pairs. Also add one card that says: "Class is boring. You lose. "
It is the "Old Maid" card and whoever ends up with it automatically loses.

How to Play:

Put students into groups of 5
One student deals the cards - 5 cards to each player. Each player must always have 5 cards in their hand.
Spread the remainder of the cards on the table, face down. Spread them out into one layer of cards, as in the childhood game of "Fish."

To begin play:

The first player asks another player if they have a match to one of his/her cards. The object is to find a pair. Always say the full name of the card.
For example: "Sandy, do you have the class favorite card: experiential learning?"

If the other player has the card, he responds "Yes, I do have the class favorite card: experiential learning " and hands his card to her.

The first player puts the pair face down on the table, draws a card from the pile, and the play moves to the right. If she does not find a pair, she picks a card from the pile and discards. Each player always has 5 cards in their hand.
Each pair is always placed face down on the table.

The next player continues the play until all the cards are gone.
To win, you must have the most pairs
YOU AUTOMATICALLY LOSE, if you are left holding the "You Lose" card.

When the game is complete, lead the class in a brainstorm of the concepts they learned on the cards. By repeating the concept on the card each time they handle it, you will find that they have a high recall of these concepts, learned through play.

SUMMARIES AS OPENINGS

I encourage you to use the idea of summaries as an opening of each class. As you move into the material for each session, summarize what the class has covered so far. This is a simple, effective way to focus the attention of your adult learners and help them to more powerfully integrate the class content.

It is fun to include the students in the process. For example, you can brainstorm with them a list of all that has been covered so far. You can make a list of topics on a flip chart and take a class vote on their personal favorite topic by each checking their 3 favorites with a marker. You can ask for a personal story from the week that would illustrate last week's concepts. All of these achieve the same underlying goal: to gently bring your adult student's attention back to the class material in a fun, interesting, involving way

Experiment with your class openings and develop your own tool kit of ideas that work in various situations. Your opening sets the tone for the class experience. A little extra care given to the class beginning will carry it a long way toward an exciting, participative experience of learning for your student.

4. Engaging Your Students

WAYS TO MAKE YOUR CLASS RELEVANT

Imagine with me for a moment. Imagine that I was to offer you a beautiful, fully ripened orange. It is an orange like no other. It is perfectly round, brilliant in color and filled up with sunlight. When I cut into this orange, it is sweet, juicy, and delicious, still warm from the tree. It is completely wonderful in every way. An amazing orange. Can you imagine it? So, now I ask you. Which would you prefer? Would you like me to continue with my description of this incredible orange? Or, would you like me to reach through the page and place it in your hand so that you can taste it for yourself?

The joy of learning is as indispensable in study as breathing is to running.

SIMONE WEIL

This is a metaphor for how your students feel about their class. It is nice to hear you talk about it and describe it in vivid detail. But, they would rather experience it for themselves. They want to take the ideas you have to offer, practice them, live them, and master them in their lives.

This is the essence of adult education, and it is the reason adults are returning to school in great numbers. Adult education now is about experience, relevance and quick understanding.

The ease of online information has made the old ways of passing information ineffective. Remember, your adult student can, anytime they please, find out the facts, history and data backup for almost any

*A wise
teacher
makes
learning
a joy.*

PROVERBS

subject online. In your classroom, your student wants to participate in learning, share their life perspective, talk directly with the experts, and move into using the new information quickly. They expect your class to be exciting, participative, creative, experiential, and inclusive. Still, as educators, we know that it is usually necessary to pass new information or data to the student. How will you do it? It is up to you to decide. You must find ways to pass critical information to your students in a way that they will receive it. If they can have fun doing it, all the better.

Here are a few basics:

Reading Assignments: In the old days you might assign reading and go back over it in class. Now it is more relevant to assume that your adult student has read and assimilated the text. Going back over assigned reading in detail is the kiss of death for adult education. Boring! Instead, especially if the reading is long or difficult, simply ask if there are any questions regarding the reading.

Begin your classroom comments with major highlights from the reading. Hearing you say it assists your auditory learner and can help all the students integrate the material better. Do not read from the book! Instead, choose major points and give live examples to bring the reading to life.

Prepare some questions from the reading to engage the students in discussion. Even with these tools, plan to spend only a short period of time on the reading. The adult learner has the book and can spend more time on the material themselves, if they so choose.

Definitions, Facts, Figures and Data: Ok, so you *can* spend time talking over terms, facts, and explaining data. But it does not create a dynamic learning experience for your student. Consider other ways to pass this material. A simple handout of definitions is a good tool and gives the student the opportunity to save it, file it, share it.

If mastery of data or definitions is critical to your subject, think of ways to engage your student in the process. Create a crossword puzzle of terms. Design a trivial pursuit game of your facts. Play a true-false game with your data.

It has been proven that fun, interactive exercises are fast and effective in transferring this kind of information to your student in a way that they can remember. They have fun doing it. For ideas in this area, look online at the wide variety of educational games websites for kids. These kid activities can be perfect for adult students when you adapt them for your needs.

The mediocre teacher tells. The good teacher explains. The superior teacher demon-strates. The great teacher inspires.

WILLIAM ARTHUR WARD

The Merits of Not Telling: Gone are the days when people would gather in the square and hang on every word of the great orator. Today, when adults give up their precious evenings or weekends to take classes, they come to participate in the process. The more you can refrain from telling them all the answers, the more exciting and dynamic your learning environment will be.

If your question is not readily understood, ask it again in another context and see if someone can answer. If it still seems difficult, ask any of your students to research the topic and report back at the next class. You may have extensive research on this subject. But, the class will be more dynamic and the results more compelling if your students arrive at their own conclusions. You can add your research information at the end, as another perspective. This inclusive teaching style makes for a lively, empowering learning experience. Better yet. ask them to do research in class on their smart phones.

ENGAGE YOUR STUDENTS WITH STORIES

Imagination is more important than knowledge.

ALBERT
EINSTEIN

For as long as there have been teachers, there have been stories. Everyone loves a good story, and it can be your best tool for conveying an idea to your student. All the great scriptures of the world use stories to teach their message and so can you. Where will you find these stories? Your own life. What better way to convey the challenges of life than to share an experience of your own? You will also find good stories in many other books.

Check online, explore YouTube, and ask other teachers what they use. This an exciting, creative way to teach. You may want to consider taking a workshop to perfect your storytelling skills or inviting a professional storyteller to visit your class.

Your ability to tell an interesting story can be a great asset in classroom discussion. Your skill will transport your students into a different mindset and a new way of thinking. Stories are a safe, interesting way for your students to reorganize information in their mind. They will look at your subject matter through fresh eyes and an imaginative approach. With good storytelling, you will be able to create an authentic conversation and encourage students to expand their views by hearing other's perspectives.

Retreats are especially good places for storytelling because there is time to do them justice. It is also fun to ask your students to act out stories for the group. When teaching about early philosophers, I like to search online for their original letters and create scripts for a reader's theater. Students each take the part of one philosopher and, as the conversation goes back and forth, the philosophers come to life in the room. Try a reader's theater in your class. It is a fun way to bring historical characters to life.

Most teachers come naturally to the art of storytelling. To be a good storyteller, you must be a good communicator and be able to edit the truth to make your point. <u>Stories convey emotion and build community in the classroom.</u> Most importantly, stories cloak information in an imaginative way that makes it easier for the student to process it and relate to it on a personal basis. For example, we can talk at length about the historical facts of the early settlers of our country. But, when we hear a story of one family and what they endured to settle the West, then we can begin to relate this period of history to our personal lives.

And so, decide. What story will you tell? Will you tell a personal story, a historical story, a grand adventure, the story of a memorable character? You have many choices. There are many wonderful stories to tell that apply to the subject you are teaching. You can find them easily online.

How to Tell a Great Story

- Set the stage: Be sure you have a proper space that is comfortable for your audience. Is it quiet and comfortable? Is the temperature and lighting right?
- Begin with a few minutes of introduction. Allow your listeners to get used to you and your voice.
- Plan your tone of voice, pacing and meaningful silences.
- Use drama. Part of the fun of listening to the story is the drama. Try to vary your voices, use gestures, and sound effects. Be creative in the telling.
- Choose a point of view. Who will the narrator of your story be? Is it you, speaking in first person? Is it an impartial observer? Is it a magical fairy story teller? Decide who is telling this story before you begin
- Visualize the story in your mind while telling it. If you can imagine it, so can your listener.
- Remember that stories are interactive, so pause for your audience to laugh or to react to your story. Give them time to think and absorb the meaning.
- Take your time. Slow down. Relax. Engage. Enjoy the telling.
- Use good pronunciation. Speak clearly and use good diction.
- Use your own style.
- Practice, practice, practice!

BLESSING THE NEWSPAPER

Another way to bring class concepts to life is to use the daily newspaper. It is fun to bring copies of the paper into the class, break the class into small groups, and ask them to find examples of the class concepts at work in the world.

Human life, from ancient time, is filled with the same kinds of struggles and passions of love, hate, joy, sorrow, faith, success, failure, politics, and war. The newspaper reflects these lessons on a daily basis. Use the newspaper yourself and point out where the class information is showing up today.

This exercise may be one of the most important additions to your class when teaching heart-centered topics. People today want to know how to apply their beliefs and values to all that is happening in our world. Front page headlines can be intimidating. It is often hard to reconcile the premium our culture sets on fame, fortune, sex, and competition with the inner qualities of patience, freedom, justice, honesty, and love.

You may find this challenging for yourself. I encourage you to step right into the news and make it your textbook for your class. When you can train yourself and your class to see the good values at work in the news and all the wonderful things that are happening and reported (usually in the back pages of the paper), you will gain strength in your understanding of life. And so will your students.

ART PROJECTS

Art projects in adult learning are not childish nor are they simply included to pass the time. Art is an important language of the heart and the imagination. By creating with your hands, you begin to create in your life. Your mind and imagination are put into service, and these art projects become symbols of change and inspiration. Use them as a way for students to express feelings and ideas so deeply hidden within that they are unaware of them.

I like to use crayons and paper, for example, in clearing emotions and old ideas. Ask each student to take a crayon and just scribble on a piece of paper, thinking of any old incident or feeling that was painful. The scribble carries the emotion from the inner heart. It can also carry old ways of thinking and living.

Once we show each other our scribbles, we then tear up our papers and throw them away. This simple art project signals that we are beginning to let go of old feelings and old ways of living. It is experienced as an energetic release by the student. I always observe a lift in the class energy and much joy after such an exercise. Students become more present and ready to learn.

There are many other uses for art projects. I encourage you to be creative in imagining how art can be used in your classroom to portray the journey of life. Once your class topic is converted into a piece of art, even a scribble, the student begins to be able to integrate new learning into their lives. Art represents ideas, feelings, and events in life itself. Working symbolically with art is an energetic way for students to create what they want or intend to change in their lives. It is a concentration or even an acceleration of their process.

Sometimes I ask students, on the first night of class, to draw a picture or symbol of what they hope to accomplish in our time together. By looking at each other's artwork, even if very simple, the students form an intuitive idea of how we will be in class together. Each student forms a clear impression of the intentions of the other.

It is fun to have students cut up magazines and make a collage of their dreams. As they create these dream maps on paper, they also begin to create their dreams in consciousness through thought, imagination and symbol. By showing their maps to their classmates,

I am not young enough to know everything

OSCAR
WILDE

To be a teacher, you must be a prophet - because you are trying to prepare people for a world of the future.

GORDON
BROWN

they begin to build community, as well as spiritual support for their dreams to come true.

It is equally powerful to use clay or even play dough to create something new in their life. When molding the clay, the student learns that it is physically possible to create something entirely new from almost nothing. This experience makes it easier for them to understand the process of their lives. Use this powerful medium to represent in the outer world what is taking place in the inner heart. Encourage students to continue using these art projects at home. For more ideas, see the art projects section, in Chapter Six.

GAMES

Games are an excellent way to pass along a lot of data. One of the great things about adult students is that they already have many answers from their personal experience. The right game can bring out their knowledge and pass lots of facts to them in a fun way.

Perhaps you put together a basket of questions about your subject matter and form two teams. Pass the basket and let the two teams compete to see who can answer the most correctly.

Perhaps you create a card game in which each card holds an idea for the class. Or a word game to teach new vocabulary. There are many websites that will help you to design a crossword or word finder games.

Simply entering the vocabulary you are teaching and some questions; the puzzle designs itself. The crossword on the next page, designed on a site called Hot Potato, is based upon the concepts in this book. Can you complete the puzzle? See the end of this chapter for the solution

Engaging Adult Learners

Complete the crossword puzzle.

Across

2   How adult students feel about being read to out of a book

3   How auditory learners like to learn

6   These bring your comments to life

Down

1   Your adult student finds it more fun to

4   Should you assume your adult student has done their homework?

5   Fun ways to teach facts and data

POETRY

*I'm not a
teacher,
but an
awakener.*

ROBERT
FROST

And then, there is poetry. Do you have the courage to use poetry as the basis for a discussion in your class? This tool is magical indeed. Great poetry is written and, therefore understood, from a highly intuitive consciousness or an unusual depth of feeling. It uses symbols, pictures, and language to convey deep truths in a few words. When carefully reading a piece of poetry, the student can begin to see his or her reflection within it. Poetry invites interpretation and deep understanding in the listener. When sharing these ideas, the entire class opens to a profound view of the world and the subjects you are teaching. Even funny poems and rhymes often have a clever wisdom to them that can be a great asset to you in your teaching methods.

It is nice if you have a controlled, safe environment in which to explore the deep dimensions of poetry together. However, in my experience, it is often true that you are working with a rollicking bunch of adults who are taking classes in a lively fashion and do not want to work with pauses and silences and deep meanings. Poetry is still a wonder to use in your class. There is a poem for any topic.

As an example, I have used the great poem *Casey at the Bat* in a class on public speaking. The colorful images and rhyme make this piece of poetry fun to read aloud when practicing diction. Another idea: use some of the great proliferation of rap poetry as a voice to be heard in classes about social order, community, diversity, or politics. Perhaps after you share a few of these, your students can be persuaded to try their hand at composing a rap poem about your class topic. Haiku is another beautiful style of poetry I have enjoyed using as a way for students to summarize the class experience.

Great poems can be used in classes dealing with women's issues, learning languages, geography, history, and so many more. My favorite is to use poetry as the hub for deep and heartfelt discussion. When exploring a piece of poetry together, students learn to express authentic feelings. They begin to intuit, think and feel for themselves more deeply than they would on their own. The class begins to be a true learning community, built upon a solid foundation of truth, personal experience, and glimpses into each other's world. Wonderful.

HOW TO USE POETRY AS A
BASIS FOR A HEART-OPENING DISCUSSION

Begin with silence. Go around the room, and ask each student to read a few lines of the poem aloud. Then lead a discussion using the questions that follow. Remind each student that in this exercise, everyone is empowered to speak truthfully and only for themselves. Cross talk is discouraged in order that everyone can speak without being challenged for their feelings or ideas. Let there be silent spaces in the discussion - times for reflection. This powerful experience is based upon Parker Palmer's work with Circles of Trust.

Days full of wanting
Let them go by without worrying that they do.
Stay where you are inside the pure, hollow note.

Your way begins on the other side. Become the sky
Take an axe to the prison wall. Escape
Walk out like someone suddenly born into color.
Do it now.

RUMI

EXAMPLE

Wild Geese
by Mary Oliver

You do not have to be good.
You do not have to walk on your knees
for a hundred miles through the desert repenting.
You only have to let the soft animal of your body
love what it loves.
Tell me about despair, yours, and I will tell you mine.
Meanwhile the world goes on.
Meanwhile the sun and the clear pebbles of the rain
are moving across the landscapes,
over the prairies and the deep trees,
the mountains and the rivers.
Meanwhile the wild geese, high in the clean blue air,
are heading home again.
Whoever you are, no matter how lonely,
the world offers itself to your imagination,
calls to you like the wild geese, harsh and exciting —
over and over announcing your place
in the family of things.

Questions:

1. What do the wild geese remind you of in your life?

2. If the soft animal of your body loves, what does it love?

3. Let the discussion evolve from here, asking any other appropriate
questions geared to stimulating personal insights and learning from this
poem. Continue until everyone feels complete. Ask students to share this
experience with each other at the end.

EXPERIENTIAL EXERCISES

The fact is, no one learns anything new from having it told to them. They can hear you describe it, but not until they begin to experience it for themselves can they truly learn its meaning. Imagine listening to someone describe how to play a good game of tennis. You can gain some good pointers for your game, but not until you get out on the court and actually try it, do you learn how to do it.

No one has ever taught anything to anybody.

CARL ROGERS

Remember the importance of experiential exercises in adult learning. Your task as a teacher is to give the adult student an experience that gives him or her a deeper understanding in life. Experience makes your classroom exciting and prepares your student to live more successfully.

How is this done? Through the body, including the vital emotions, experiences, activities, physical sensations, kinesthetic movements, and energies of change. Physical experiences are the doorway to success and more effective living. The senses are especially suited to experiences that educate the whole person.

Your task is to create an experience for the student that accomplishes this. Where to begin? Consider your subject matter. Ask yourself, what can the body do to act out mastery of this subject?

If you are teaching a communication course, the choice is easy: create an exercise in which the student must step up and communicate. If you are teaching a French class, take your students out to visit a French restaurant. Require that your students speak only French to the waiter.

If you are teaching a class about relationship, create experiential exercises that open the heart so that the student begins to experience love. Go around the room and ask each student to name something that he/she truly loves. Feel the experience of love in the classroom.

47

"Teaching" is a catch-all phrase whose actual meaning is instruction, and only accounts for 1/5 of learning. Facilitation promotes the other 4/5 of the process of learning, which takes place within the individual.

MICHAEL BERGER

Experiential exercises touch into the authentic self. In life and in the classroom, when we stop and appreciate what we are doing, we feel better about ourselves; we open up to new ideas for doing things better, and we feel more connected with each other.

Remember, the language of the heart is color, symbolism, music, art, poetry, imagination, visualization, intuition. How can you use your eyes, your ears, your sense of touch, your nose, your physical being to experience greater understanding? How can you use these tools to create experiential exercises that help you teach new ideas?

The question to ask is: what bodily experience is most helpful to teach this information? Plan to actually do something - write, dance, walk, move around the room, hug, shake hands, anything that helps live out the concept you are teaching. Experience is powerful and gives students a new way of thinking that they will never forget.

ASKING QUESTIONS

Asking the provocative question is a teaching tool as old as Socrates. It still works. If you have a knack for asking interesting questions, your classes will never be boring. Use questions to rescue the discussion from a trite conversation based upon nothing important.

Students like to talk things over with each other and so it is necessary to provide time for general give and take conversation. You must decide, however, how much idle chatter you will tolerate.

You will want to do something when false values start to show up as truth in student conversations. For example, in a recent class, one student was complaining to the rest about the price of groceries. Everyone seemed to be interested in this discussion, and it went on for a few minutes, with other students joining in with their own complaints. The problem for me, and for you, in such a situation, is that this conversation does not improve life for anyone. By giving the class permission to begin to share worries, fears, and negativity in your class, you become responsible for the discouraging viewpoints they may adopt.

It is up to you to pull this conversation back to a more heart-centered, productive discussion. Adult education is for the purpose of making life easier, more successful, more fulfilling. Encourage your students to take the facts of their world and make them work for success. Possible questions to ask the class:

Life is a series of lessons that must be lived to be understood

EMERSON

> Why does this situation create anxiety for you?
>
> What would you say is the bigger issue at work here?
>
> If we were to think that these rising prices are actually doing us a service, what do you think it would be?

Don't be afraid to go deep with your questioning. It is your role in the class to stimulate these discussions. In personal development classes, the students are presenting you with material for their life expansion. Step right into the topics they pick and apply your curriculum material to their subject.

As a cautionary note, however, do not let the student do the same to you. Sometimes, we have a student who likes to play "stump the teacher." This one likes to ask you tough questions or take the class on a long detour with questions that have no clear answer.

Remember you do not have to have all the answers. The best response is to turn the question back onto the student who asked it: "That's an interesting question, Larry. What do you think about that?" This will provoke a little more discussion, and then you can bring the group gently back to focus. "This is interesting but to keep to our time commitments, let's turn to our assignments for this week."

MEDITATION AND VISUALIZATION

Meditation and visualizations are not tools for passing data to your students. But they are powerful tools for touching real emotions and teaching through experience. Scientists have proven for years that when we imagine ourselves doing something in detail, our bodies feel that they have actually done it.

Athletes use visualization to perfect their skiing or their golf swing or their field goals. Visualization builds skills. So, you can use guided visualization to give your students the experience of what you are teaching.

If you are talking about making peace in the world, for example, it is powerful to guide the student through the process of forgiving someone in their life. If a student is learning to be a better communicator, you can guide them through a visualization of being a patient listener. If a student is seeking health and well-being, you can guide them through the visualization of a vibrant experience of health. You can use visualization to practice new behaviors, learn new skills, heal wounds, change old habits. The power of the mind, used in this way, is a powerful tool for change. When leading these kinds of exercises, open your heart, talk slowly and handle your students gently. This is profound work.

Man's mind,
once stretched by a new idea,
never regains its original dimensions.

OLIVER WENDELL HOLMES

WHAT DO WE HAVE TO TEACH EACH OTHER?

In this chapter, we have introduced ideas for engaging your adult student. These are some of the basic ways to approach your class and pass along information to them effectively. As you prepare your class, examine each curriculum section and create new ways for passing information to your students that are involving and fun. Keep in mind that you can try stories, examples from the newspaper, experiential exercises, art projects, games, visualization, and deep questions to bring about the perfect opportunity for each student's optimal experience.

We will be discussing these in more detail later in this book. But before we do, there is another step in this process of heart-centered teaching to consider first. Each adult student holds wisdom they have acquired over a lifetime. How will you evoke this inner wisdom and bring it into the conversation in your classroom? What do we have to teach other? This is the topic we will consider next.

CROSSWORD PUZZLE SOLUTION

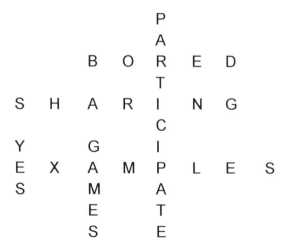

5. Drawing Out Student Wisdom

MINING THE WEALTH OF KNOWLEDGE IN YOUR CLASS

One of the most powerful concepts to remember when teaching adults is that the students are the true curriculum for your class. No matter what the class subject matter is, it has little importance unless it can be a valued contribution to everyday life. Each experience, challenge, accomplishment, question - all of these are the reasons we are here doing this work.

It is important to prepare and understand the wisdom of the material you are teaching. But once you step through the classroom door, the great school of life is in session. Each student is on their own path and has their own questions. Each student brings with them answers for everyone else.

As the teacher, it is important to remember that this class is called together on purpose. All that each student wants to learn for their greatest good can happen here. The inner wisdom of each student is part of this complex experience.

Often, adult learners are confident and comfortable enough to share themselves with the class. If not, it is your responsibility to draw them out. I do not mean that we need to know all about their lives, and the great stories of their history they hold about themselves. Rather, I mean that we are seeking to know what makes them unique,

If a teacher is indeed wise, he does not bid you to enter the house of his wisdom, but rather leads you to the threshold of your mind.

KAHLIL GIBRAN

*He who
does not
know
one
thing,
knows
another.*

*KENYAN
PROVERB*

the personal wisdom that each holds. We have much to learn from every person here. As the class comes back together at the start of each session, listen carefully to the conversations going on. Give time for each to speak into the room and share about the intervening time period since the last meeting. You can let this happen casually or ask a leading question such as "What's happened that is good and new since we were together last?"

All that we have discussed so far in this book is part of drawing out student wisdom. The shy soul will emerge in the right environment when there is space available for this to happen. For this reason, it is important for you to carefully consider the spaces you are creating for class. Do this physically. Just as we do when teaching children, we find that adult learners enjoy changing spaces during class.

You may wish to set up one part of the room for the whole group to sit together for discussion. You may wish to use the the hallway as a place where student projects, visuals, and papers are hung for reading. Another space can be used for break-out groups. Perhaps a more quiet space is available for meditation or silence.

Don't worry that you are using class time to move and get reoriented while the group settles down into a new space. This is a valuable social opportunity for adult learners which they treasure. By moving around, you provide the opportunity for the body to stretch and unwind a little, so that it is easier for students to concentrate when you begin again.

TOOLS FOR DISCUSSION

Many times the success and effectiveness of the class depend upon the value of the class discussion. There is a science and an art to leading and facilitating meaningful discussions for adult learners. Here are a few tools to explore. This is one area, however, where you will have to step into the situation and try some of these ideas before you find tools that are suited to your teaching style.

1. Open-ended questions

True learning must be experienced or discovered by the student for lasting progress. There is good news and bad news for you as the teacher. On one hand, you will not be expected to have all the answers. On the other hand, you must be secure and certain enough in yourself to allow the class conversation to unfold, without knowing where it will lead.

What we know for sure is that the discussion will be exactly the way it is for the deepest learning of this particular class. You need not be nervous asking open-ended questions and letting the student's responses flow through unchartered waters. Here are some examples of open-ended questions to keep in mind for class discussions:

- Have you ever had an experience similar to our author's experience? Can you tell us about it?
- What did you learn from this experience?
- When do you feel happy (or sad, or fearful)?
- What do you do about it?
- Does this reading remind you of something in your life?
- Can you tell us more about your example?
- Why is this important to you?
- I am not sure why that is so. Why do you think it is so?

One doesn't discover new lands without consenting to lose sight of the shore for a very long time.

ANDRE GIDE

2. Unlearning

Genius without education is like silver in the mine.

BEN FRANKLIN

An old Zen story tells of a great teacher who sat high on the mountain in his humble hut, and a seeker came to learn from him. The two sat down at the table, and the teacher began to prepare tea. The seeker was excited and began to tell the great teacher all about his life. The teacher began to pour tea into the student's cup while he talked. And as the seeker continued to talk, the teacher continued to pour until the tea overflowed the cup and spilled all over the table.

Astonished, the seeker leapt up and said, "What are you doing? It is too full." The teacher responded, "Yes, just as you are too full. There is no room in you for new ideas because you are so full of your own."

Especially with experienced students, it often seems that they are so full of their own ideas that there is no room for any new thoughts. It is important to guide the class in releasing the old cluttered ideas and make room for new understanding. Try expanding discussions by introducing imagination into your discussion questions.

For example, you can create an imaginary world where old concepts are no longer valid. You might say: "Let's suppose for a moment that money is no object. What kind of work would you do?" or "Let's imagine for a moment that only women could be leaders. How do you think the world would change?" or "What if everything you did was already forgiven. How would you feel differently about your life?"

Another excellent tool for unlearning is a panel discussion. When participating in a panel on a deeply personal topic, students will find that they, by necessity, begin to let go of the strong hold they have on their opinions. For example, if you create a panel discussion on the death penalty, it will be a profound experience for each student to hear their classmates express opposite views. Or, you can hold a panel discussion of the newspaper headlines. One thing is certain; each person is different. Listening to the wide range of attitudes, students begin to broaden their minds and their perspectives.

Sometimes a ritual can be effectively used to symbolize unlearning. I like to do a cleansing of the hands ritual at the door of the class. Ask your students to repeat a lovely quote or affirmation dealing with the willingness to have a beginner's mind.

Or ask students to write down everything on their mind at the beginning of class. Then ask them to tear up these papers and throw away the pieces or safely burn them to symbolize the mind clearing.

If you are desperate to unclog the the discussions, set your watch for 3 minutes and tell everyone that they have to all talk at once for the next 3 minutes. They can say anything they want to, but they cannot stop for 3 minutes. It is important for you to do this too, as a model for how it is done.

With everyone talking at once, it will create quite a din in the room. When you call time, you will find before you a group of smiling, emptied-out students who are present, energized, and ready for the next part of the class.

Creativity is a type of learning in which the teacher and the student are located in the same individual.

ARTHUR KOESTLER

3. Silence

One of the great tools of class discussion is silence. It took me years to learn this. Silence in the class is so powerful, I urge you to master this tool sooner rather than later. The point is you must be comfortable to allow the class to fall into periods of silence. It might be that there has been a very deep or emotional discussion. The class goes silent to make sense of it individually and consider a response. It may be that you have asked a probing question and students are sorting it out in their heads, unsure of their response. If this type of silence goes on too long, rephrase the question. Almost every time, one of your class leaders will become uncomfortable and speak. This starts discussion rolling again.

It is important to relax and wait. Some will speak; the silence will return; then more will speak and so on. When you are comfortable with the silence, the class will go deeper and deeper on its own. How long is too long? That is up to you. I have waited many times in silence for five to ten minutes with good result.

4. Listening and connecting to the previous point

Imagine that your classroom is a movie set and everything said there is scripted for the highest learning and deepest understanding of everyone, including you. This idea is very close to the truth. You must be present. If you have busyness going on in your life, take fifteen minutes or so before class to write down all that you are thinking. Make a list of all that you will do later. For the short space of your class, let the paper hold those ideas, so that you can be present.

As the discussion unfolds, listen deeply to the concerns that are being expressed. Ask yourself, what truth is this person seeking? You will find themes begin to reveal themselves in your student discussion. Are they seeking greater hope? To be more loving? Are they seeking to find greater love for themselves? Are they grieving the loss of people or jobs? Are there things in the way that makes it hard for them to find balance in their lives? The answers revealed in the class discussion will guide you in knowing which direction to take in the class.

Most importantly, as the class continues, you will be able to refer back to specific comments by individuals that were relevant to your topics. This tracking of the discussion helps the students to feel certain about your direction and to understand the importance of every contribution made in the conversation.

GROUP DYNAMICS IN YOUR CLASSROOM
Common Roles in Group Behavior

LEADER
This person is a natural leader and has a strong drive to take charge, and manage the group. Taking the lead can only occur with the group's spoken or unspoken permission. Often, one or more leaders will emerge in the group. The group informally decides who will lead.

ELDER
Although not actively leading, this member is believed to have the most experience or talent. The group will look to its elder for wisdom. Usually, he/she holds veto power over a group decision.

GATEKEEPER
Keeps the group on task and openly monitors time schedules, assignments, and decisions.

BUTTERFLY
A real people lover whose motivation is to have a social experience, regardless.

REBEL
Does not conform to group behavior or decision making. Sometimes the rebel can splinter a group by encouraging members to go off on their own.

NEGOTIATOR
This person is process oriented and interested in moderation and compromise.

HEALER
The earth mother of the group. She feels responsible for taking care of the members.

WORKHORSE
This member is willing to do the work of ten people in order to make the group run smooth, including typing up the contact list, making copies, bringing snacks, or whatever it takes.

DIALOGUE

Dialogue is a wonderful tool for teaching adults. It takes practice. For thousands of years, it has been effectively used as a conversational way to explore truth. Dialogue works well with philosophical subjects, where no one knows all the answers. It elicits knowledge from the students rather than passing knowledge to them. Since every subject has its philosophical dimension, every subject is suitable for dialogue some of the time.
To use Dialogue in your classroom;

Choose a topic that is of genuine importance to the students.

1. Honestly tell the students that you will facilitate the dialogue, but that the truth is already contained within each person here. By carefully listening to each other, we will hear the truth emerge. In a dialogue, we share our ideas. It is not a discussion in which we have a conversation.

2. Begin with silence for a few moments. Then ask the question for the dialogue. All thoughts and feelings on the subject are welcome.

3. Participants do not react, debate, or attempt to answer each other's question. Each relates instead to the dialogue itself. Everyone questions and everyone answers. The truth is at the center of the dialogue, not in anyone's head.

4. As an instructor, you will participate only about 5% of the time. Since you are well versed on the subject matter, you can step in and guide the dialogue a little with a new questions, if it seems to be going off track. However, do not attempt to fill the silences. All must be heard. Much silence is necessary.

5. With dialogue, participants do not interview, nor do they debate. Rather they listen deeply within, share their inspirations on the subject, and ask rhetorical questions. Victory is not the goal of the dialogue but rather truth.

6. The teacher who uses the tool of dialogue must possess a set of moral qualities, including honesty, respect, humility and even a kind of restraint.

6. Learning through Experience

HOW TO CREATE EXPERIENTIAL EXERCISES THAT WORK

Who can forget the taste of a crisp apple, the smell of bread baking, the warmth of the sun, the sound of a baby laughing? Our senses bring our experiences to us in a heightened way in so many areas of life. It is certainly true in the classroom. Your task is to create a physical, sensory experience for the student that gives them the understanding and practice of new ideas. As they experience their new learning, they acquire a personal mastery of these new concepts. The difference between being a good teacher and a great teacher largely depends upon the quality of the experiential practice you offer to your adult student.

I hear and I forget. I see and I remember. I do and I understand

CHINESE PROVERB

Where to begin? Ask yourself: if students were to use their hands, their senses, their movements, to live out what you are teaching, what would they do? For example, if you are teaching history, how can your students act out the events you are discussing? If you are teaching literature, could the students do a readers' theater or debate from the point-of-view of their favorite writer? If you are teaching language, could the class go on a field trip or to a restaurant and use their new language skills? If you are teaching emotional topics, could the students counsel each other? If you are teaching art, can the students try their hands at various techniques?

Perhaps more challenging, when teaching spiritual topics, what can your body do that would speak the language of the soul? Remember, the language of the soul is color, symbolism, music, art, poetry, imagination, visualization, intuition. How can you use your eyes, your ears, your sense of touch, your nose, your physical being to experience the inner world?

In this chapter, we will be discussing ways to engage your students in this type of transformative learning. Throughout this chapter, you will find specific ideas for experientials to try in your classroom. Be brave and experiment with what works best for your students. You will be surprised to see the power and sense of excitement that builds with the use of excellent experiential exercises.

CREATING EXCELLENT EXPERIENTIAL EXERCISES
Here are some guiding questions for creating experiential exercises:

1. Give some careful thought to the experience you are creating. Are you looking for an experience of peace while being alone and quiet, or peace in the midst of noise and chaos?

2. What will serve the student best? Consider what experience you are creating carefully.

3. Can a student do it alone? Does there need to be someone else to assist? How many people will it take to be powerful and effective?

4. How physical do you want it to be? Do you want to use a symbol for this experience or do you want the student to act it out?

5. Do you need to bring in a guest or an expert to make it more real?

6. Does it require a change of location to be effective? Imagine the most real circumstance and try to replicate it.

7. What materials will this experience require? The more real you can make it, the more effective it will be.

WHAT SIZE OF SMALL GROUP WILL YOU USE?

One person: Individual work
Private, good for inner understanding, and tender or sensitive topics.

Two people: Partners
Sharing with another can validate the student's experience and ideas,
Provides a detailed look at another's life in order to see one's own more clearly.

Three to Six people: Small Group
Provides an opportunity for presenting ideas to others to strengthen confidence.
Creates the opportunity for personal breakthroughs with group support. Group
energy can inspire individuals to expanded thinking, encourage creativity, and
provide fun bonding experiences in class. Not a safe environment for deep
personal sharing unless the group knows and likes each other well.

More than 6 people: Group
A less safe environment for sharing ideas, but great for experiential work that
involves brainstorming, movement, consensus building, or high energy work.

EMBODIMENT OF THE CLASS LEARNING

When the students embody the class material, they live it, they own it, it belongs
to them. They physically experience the ideas you are offering. For example, one
favorite is the trust walk. In this exercise, the student wears a blindfold and their
partner guides them along a fifteen minute walk out-of-doors. This exercise
demands that the student trust their partner to guide them. Afterwards, a class
discussion will reveal all the inner fears that must be released in this exercise.
Students find a true reference for what it feels like to trust, an experience they
never forget. From this exercise, they can begin to trust in other areas of life.

RITUAL

Ritual is an important tool for teachers. It can be as simple as the way the class assembles each time, the way the class session always opens or closes, or the way someone is appreciated for their work. Ritual gives meaning to ordinary events, brings a quiet certainty to the classroom and strengthens the sense of community.

Ritual is a formal way of depicting in the outer world what is happening in the inner world. When you remember this definition, it becomes easier to create powerful ritual experiences. Think of what you ritual is symbolizing and try to replicate or enact it in the class.

For example, if the occasion is one of advancement ,graduation, or moving into a new phase of life, it is powerful to include walking, stepping, crossing over a bridge or walking a path in your ritual. Imagine rose petals, confetti, glitter, stones, candles, fabric for paths; sticks, ribbons, paper, wood for thresholds to step over.

For completion of studies or achieving some mastery, think of anointing, crowning, or blessing with such simple tools as water or scented oil. You may do this for the student; students may do this for each other, or the students may bless themselves.

If the occasion is one of coming together for workshops , weekends or retreats, think of ways to symbolize community. Consider an altar, group drawings, or gathering of outdoor materials to create a beautiful center point in the room. Your topic will drive the materials for this. Choose things that represent the group: candles, vining plants, fresh flowers, shells, sacred symbols, colorful fabrics, leaves, branches, objects of beauty.

A simple drink of water poured for each student from a single glass pitcher can create community or common goals for the class and be a profound experience for all.

I encourage you to incorporate ritual into your class. Sometimes it takes bravery to step into these ideas. The important thing to remember is that by using rituals in your class, you speak to the deeper side of your students. The human spirit loves ceremony, symbolism, and the inner side of life. You invoke this richly with careful use of ritual.

OPENING THE HEART

One of the greatest experiences you can offer your students is the opportunity to open their hearts. We live in a world where many do not feel safe to open their hearts, and speak their personal truth. Often our lives are so busy, it seems we don't take the time to patiently listen to others. No life is complete if the real, individual truth of us cannot emerge and be told. Just speaking what is on our heart makes our life feel important and complete.

The heart is the great doorway to the soul. Once this door opens, all the power and miracles of the inner world become more real. We are more essentially ourselves when we are feeling our way, trusting our inner guidance, and intuition. It is not possible to express all of our powerful capabilities through the tiny organ of the brain. We must engage our whole being, our senses, our imagination, intuition, instinct, and inner knowing. This happens when we open our hearts.

Opening the heart occurs when we bring our attention to the quality of love. It has been proven that people are happier living alone if they have a pet that they can love. Loving parents open their

If your heart acquires strength, you will be able to remove blemishes from others without thinking evil of them.

GANDHI

We shall never learn to feel and respect our calling and destiny until we have taught ourselves to consider everything as moonshine, compared with the education of the heart.

SIR
WALTER
SCOTT

hearts when speaking of their children. Falling in love is powerful because we see another through the eyes of the heart. Our heart intuits the true beauty of the one we love.

The heart is the doorway through which spiritual beauty and truth can flow into this world. It is the place where we communicate with ourselves and our profound inner knowing. It is the seat of deep spiritual practice

How to guide your students to the experience of opening their heart? To do this, you must know your students. Great teachers can evoke a heart opening experience by playing the right piece of music or reciting the right piece of poetry. Usually, when a student tells a touching story or has tears during class, the hearts of their fellow students will open. Our hearts open when we experience the inner truth of another in an honest way.

I discourage you from telling sad stories about helpless or victimized people or children. There is nothing empowering about these stories. As a teacher, it is important that you firmly hold your class as a place of personal empowerment. We are all strong, powerful beyond measure and capable of creating our own lives. We are, of course, compassionate with those less fortunate. It is a weak tool to use pity to open your student's hearts.

Rather, try this experiential. Go around the classroom and ask each student to name something that they love in their life. It could be their child, a sunset, a good meal, anything they love. When everyone has spoken, including you, go around again. And, again. Try to go around at least five times. As this exercise continues, you will feel the heart of the class open. There is no need to ask the students to do anything or decide anything or commit to anything once the heart opens. The heart itself will guide them.

PONDERING

Pondering is an activity of the soul. To use pondering as an experiential exercise opens up the opportunity to deeply consider and discuss important issues and ideas. You might use a koan (as the Buddhist tradition uses) to evoke an experience of deep sharing. You might pass out a quotation or paragraph from a famous writer and ask your students to consider it. The question might be: " What guidance does this offer for my life?"

Giving time to ponder ideas such as this, in silence, without input from you, allows the inner teacher to emerge for each student. Once they begin to find a new personal perspective from pondering, they will learn to use this tool for the rest of their lives as a method of self-discovery and wisdom. Parker Palmer, in his book *To Know as We are Known*, offers great guidance in using poetry and art in the classroom to encourage this kind of inner pondering of the soul.

I was thrown out of college for cheating on the metaphysics exam. I looked into the soul of the boy next to me.

WOODY ALLEN

HUMOR

As long as your class is sitting in heavy, emotionally dense energy, there can be no real learning. The heaviness means that they are attached to old ideas. If you are not willing to laugh at an idea, you cannot change it. So, humor works well to lift the class to a new way of thinking.

Humor has its own rules. Do not poke fun at a student, even if you feel it is harmless. If the class senses any ridicule or interprets your remarks as belittling to any one of them, the entire class will turn against you. So, this is a cautionary note about using humor in any way that diminishes any student. If you are careful, you can poke

*Every
real
thought
on every
real
subject
knocks
the wind
out of
somebody
or other.*

OLIVER
WENDELL
HOLMES

fun at yourself. Students enjoy this when it is well done, and it seems to rebalance the class sometimes. You must avoid any humor related to politics, religion, sex, abortion, race, sexual preference or any other controversial topic.

The best use of humor is to be willing to be humorous about life itself. If you take issues lightly, it will lift the class and create an atmosphere in which change and growth can happen.

RELEASE FROM INTENSITY

Sometimes a class needs a release from intensity. You can define intensity in many ways. It may be a sad story that takes the energy of the class right down. It can be a deeply moving moment of joy or love or worry about current affairs, Perhaps it is an experience of walking through old issues of a discussion about family members. It can come up suddenly, from a variety of ways. Keep a few tried and true tricks up your sleeve for release from intensity.

One idea is to use sincere words of blessing for the situation that puts it in a positive light. For example, you might say, "Let's just hold this family in our hearts and know that this all turns out well for them." A good, sincere affirmation such as this will often be all that is needed to lift the class up.

Another approach is to make an effort to summarize the discussion in some logical way. For example, you might say: 'Well, we know that there are many wonderful service organizations working on this situation, and we have already identified 12 interested people who want to help. So, it looks as if there is sufficient assistance in place for this family to have the support they need to take the next steps." When you help the class find some logic in it, they will regain their balance and bring their attention back to class without continuing to worry about the topic.

Other times, only some sort of release exercise will do the trick. Try pairing up in partners and let the student say all that they wish to their partner. The partner listens quietly without commenting or offering an opinion. The partner simply listens. When the student is complete, the partner says only "I understand" or alternatively, "I hear you." Choose the response depending on your circumstance. Then change places and give the partner the opportunity to do the same. Another idea is to ask the students to write down their issue on a piece of paper and tear it up or burn it in a fireproof pan or bowl.

To release the intensity, call a break afterwards so that the students can get up, move around, and change the energy of the classroom. Playing some offbeat music during break also helps to clear the air.

The only person who is educated is the one who has learned how to learn and change.

CARL ROGERS

BREAKS

Keep your eye on the clock, watch for restlessness or boredom, and call regular breaks. How important are breaks? More important than almost anything else you do. Breaks serve an importance for the adult learner that far surpasses what you might expect. Breaks honor the body. It is an opportunity to stretch, move around, use the restroom and, let's face it, have a break from having to listen to you.

Not that you are not a great teacher. Not that the class is not good. The adult learner is already an expert in their own world. They already have their own view. It is important to give regular breaks so that they can recover themselves, and regain their power in a personal way. Call breaks every hour or every 1 1/2 hours.

Good teachers must primarily be enthusiasts. Like writers, painters, and priests, they must have a sense of vocation - a deeply-rooted unsentimental desire to do good.

NOEL
COWARD

Recently, I have seen leaders in meetings and classes call for a short "bio break." This is shorthand for "We have so much to do that we don't really want to give a break, but we know we have to let you use the restroom sometimes." Everything about this works against your intentions for your class.

Breaks are a way to honor the student in a sincere way, give a voice to the body, allow the class energies to rebalance, wake up the student and set priorities straight. We are, after all, human beings before we are students or teachers.Breaks bring us back to ourselves.

Breaks fill another very important role: providing an opportunity for social interaction of the students. You will see the animation and new enthusiasm that can come over a class during breaks. We are social animals, and your students will be more comfortable in their own skin when there is time for them to interact with each other.

THE POWER OF FOOD

There are breaks, and then there are breaks with food. The atmosphere of your classes expands exponentially when food is provided for breaks. I have had this proven to me so many times that I have lost count of the successes with food.

There are those who will say "We are intelligent, busy people. We don't need to waste the time and money on class snacks." These people are wrong. Why? Because providing food is a great demonstration of love for your students. It honors all the busy adults who forgot breakfast, or skipped lunch, or did not get home for dinner or who just get hungry. It brings us together and gives the class a common task that creates bonding in the group.

Students often get excited about this and decide among themselves to take turns bringing food. This is a great turn of events for you. Time and space will dictate what is appropriate food. Full meals are not a good idea and you may want to limit messy foods, or things that take time to prepare. I encourage you to consider the beauty of your presentation. It is an opportunity to touch the heart of the student. Offering chips still in the bag or cheese still in the wrappers is almost worse than no food at all.

Bring healthy, attractive snacks that make your students' lives better, not worse. Even a pretty bowl of almonds will please the class and provide a good balance of protein, carbohydrate, and fat to satisfy the appetite. Of course, have water for everyone. Other drinks are optional. I personally do not offer coffee, soda or sweets because I believe the caffeine and sugar make it hard for my students to be present and focused on the work we are doing together.

I took a course in speed-reading and was able to read War and Peace *in 20 minutes. It's about Russia.*

WOODY ALLEN

MUSIC, POETRY AND ART

When considering experiential learning tools, there are endless possibilities with the use of art, music, and poetry. Our adult lives are often so busy and stressed that artistic, creative expressions can take a back seat to the press of daily living. The classroom is the perfect environment for adult students to explore their own perceptions through these exercises. You may find some students hesitant to do experiential exercises of this kind. Your success depends upon your own sense of calm, nonjudgmental attitude and overall attitude that it is fun and easy. Here are a few pointers for creating these kinds of exercises for your classes.

MUSIC

It is the supreme art of the teacher to awaken joy in creative expression and knowledge.

ALBERT EINSTEIN

The use of music is powerful in many ways. You can use it to set the tone, change the mood, create a background, center the attention of the class, make a point, or open the hearts of the students. Use it in combination with any quiet exercise because it taps into the right brain side of things and encourages students to work more creatively and intuitively.

I will never forget a great class I took with Jeanne Houston, who put on opera music at top volume at the end of the class to celebrate the powerful new realizations we had learned. The strength of the vocals and the uplifting music created an overwhelming joy in the room. Take a tip from Jeanne and pick out music to transport your students into new sensations and experiences.

It's fun to ask your students to participate through singing or even dancing. I taught one class that, whenever the afternoons became long and warm, they would ask for lively music and would get up and dance for a few minutes. It was fun and a source of such laughter that made our class experience truly special. To warm up in the morning, you might try putting on some music with a good rhythm and ask your students to stretch, move, or dance.

I think it is less effective to ask students to sit and listen to the lyrics of a recorded song. No matter how lovely the song is, a group setting is too dynamic to expect students to find meaning in the words of recorded music. Listening to lyrics can only work well when they are sung live.

Singing, chanting, rounds - all kinds of singing are fun and make the class special. If they have to sing along with a recording, well, okay. It comes in a distant second to a live song leader. Even a live song leader who does it badly is better, in most cases. Experiment with music and see how powerful it can be in your classroom.

Singing and dancing are valuable as kinesthetic opportunities to engage the breath, energy, and body in dynamic movement. They help to process, integrate and enhance mental and intuitive learning. In doing so, students become complete with whatever has come before and are more open to whatever learning comes next.

The only way round is through.

ROBERT FROST

POETRY

We have already discussed the power of poetry in using dialogue in your class. However, poetry is also a thoughtful idea for experiential exercises. Poetry works because it is a way to say what otherwise cannot be said. Through poetry, feelings, ideas, and truths are conveyed beyond the words of the poem.

In almost every class I teach, I distribute a poem of some sort, based upon the content of the class itself. By reading it aloud to the class, I can offer the essence of my intention for the class, without having to lay it out in detail. I encourage you to trust this process, and let some things go unexplained. Poetry will do the rest for you in a beautiful way.

Poetry, by its very nature as fine art, tends to express a great depth of meaning and feeling in a very condensed, concentrated way. It elicits an extraordinary depth of response in the student who reads, hears, or creates it. Used appropriately, it can lead a student into levels of understanding and feeling far beyond ordinary limits. It can change his whole attitude toward the subject at hand.

It is fun to ask your students to write their own poems. They can do this together or alone. Just a few lines, to portray an idea, can create a unique experience for everyone.

I like to ask students to write a Haiku. This form of Japanese poetry is easy to do and has a formula to it, which is 3 lines with 5-7-5 syllables: line one has 5, line two has 7, line three has 5. You can find a complete explanation online.

Pass out an instruction sheet to the students and provide some pretty paper to hold their poem. This type of experiential can create memorable results in your classroom. Use it to give students a chance to summarize their learning experience in a personal way.

A Haiku:

Change

Winds are blowing now
Scattering old tired ideas
A new moon rises

ART

Uses of art in the classroom are too many to list. So, consider not what you will do for an art project, but why you will do it. Is your teaching topic very personal to the student? Have you completed an intensive module with the group? Are you dealing with difficult ideas that are hard to summarize?

Have you had a serious discussion that touches the student's values or lifestyle deeply? Is your group at odds in their opinions on a subject? Are you working with global ideas or visions for a new way of life? Are you interested in awakening the student's intuitive understanding rather than their mental comprehension of your subject? If you have answered "Yes" to any of these, then choose an art project for your class.

Remember the childhood experiences many have had. Many were judged by their teachers or ridiculed by their siblings, when they attempted art. So, you may find some students hesitate. Here is my best advice: don't ask them to draw or paint anything. Instead, give them easy assignments where there is no right or wrong way to do it. Easy, easy, easy. Approach lightheartedly and with humor.

Art is powerful and highly effective as a teaching tool. If you use it successfully, it can also be an opportunity for your adult student to rise above old wounds and ideas that they are not creative. Everyone is creative.

This is what learning is. You suddenly understand something you've understood all your life, but in a new way.

DORIS LESSING

Here are some ideas for using art experiences in your class:

To summarize a long chapter, module or weekend on one topic:
Spread out one long sheet of paper and provide many creative materials: markers, crayons, colored paper, glue, glitter, ribbons, etc. Ask the students to use these materials to express their ideas about the subject. They are to do this all together, without talking, each expressing themselves any way they choose.

When complete, stand back and look over the collective expression of this class. They will be pleased with their results. Discuss the process afterward. This works great for the close of a long session to bring the group together.

To stimulate class discussion and creativity
Pass out crayons and something to color during class discussions. I

75

like to use mandalas that I download from the Internet. As the discussion unfolds and the students color, they click into their intuitive, creative side and become more open to sharing ideas, collaboration, and problem-solving. They can talk and color, talk and color, and new ideas begin to flow.

To set goals for the new year or to create ideas on a new subject
Bring in old magazines and large sheets of paper with scissors and glue sticks. Ask the students to create a collage of their ideas on a subject. Ask the students to present their ideas as visual reports, by using these materials.

For special occasions, ceremonies or completions
Ask the students to create their own arch to walk under or threshold to cross. Provide colored paper, balloons, glitter, paint, and other supplies to use.

To realize their talents and brilliance
Bring in some clay and ask them to create a representation of themselves.

To learn creative problem solving
Give each a few sheets of aluminum foil and ask them to create a solution to a problem or an answer to a question.

What do all art projects have in common? They all tap into the inner genius of the student. Rather than just acquiring a mental idea, they begin to experience it through art: they begin to incorporate it as an experience of life. Using art as a teaching tool give you the chance to touch the whole person and fully integrate the learning experience on many levels.

ROLE PLAYING

Before we leave this chapter on experiential learning, I would like to offer a final word on role playing. If art projects help to give the adult student an experience of your subject matter, role playing does this even more.

By taking on the persona of another, the student's understanding of that person and the subject expands exponentially. It also can bring out the inner actor or actress in a most entertaining way and make for memorable classes. In my experience, adults have less resistance to this kind of work than art projects. Give it a try!

ROLE PLAYING IDEAS

- If you are teaching philosophy, world history, government, or any topic with various authority figures, assign each student to portray one of these figures. Hold a mock debate, a living room conversation, a panel, etc. Each student speaks for their assigned character.

- If you are teaching relationship subjects, mediation, communication, or any topic with personal relationships involved, assign each student to take the role of one of the people involved. Hold a mock courtroom, conversation, or just one-on-one private conversations between these figures.

- Use the Fish Bowl approach and ask a few students to play their role while the class sits around them observing. By bringing this level of expression into the classroom, you will provide your students with a new richness in their learning experience.

EXERCISES THAT WORK

Set up a mock environment and have the students walk through the situation as if they were acting it out in real life.

Create a physical exercise that gives the student a chance to do what you are talking about in class. For example, if you are teaching how to balance your schedule, teach the students to balance in a yoga posture by standing on one foot.

Create a symbolic ritual for your subject.

Use art projects to retain the class learning. At the end of a discussion, put out a big piece of paper with markers, glitter, crayons. Ask the class to come together to create a composite art drawing or collage of what the class ideas mean in their lives. Do this in silence. Afterward, invite all to admire their creation.

Use music to express class emotions. When feelings run high, put on some lively music and encourage everyone to get up and dance. When serious discussion is underway, put on some soft music for background.

Offer coloring as a way to open the mind and encourage creative thinking. Provide coloring pages and crayons for students to use during class.

Role playing. Ask students to take different parts of a current or historical situation. Put the key characters together and let them teach the class.

Field trips for reality checks. Take your class on outings to visit the real people and real places involved with what you are discussing in class.

Laugh. Ask your students to bring in a joke to tell on a class subject. Teach them that laughing is healthy and a good way to learn o see the other side of things.

Games are always great. Figure out ways to create a game out of a subject that would otherwise be detailed and boring. Multiple choice, quiz games, treasure hunts, puzzles: they all work.

7. The Secret at the Center

TRUSTING THE HEART OF YOUR CLASS

An interesting dynamic takes place in a class that is taught from the heart. Even though the subject may be very practical, even though the students are adults and begin the class as strangers, there is an intangible quality that enters into a heart-centered classroom. Because a sense of trust is built in the room, students are more genuine and honest with each other. Students feel safe to be themselves and to risk trying new behaviors.

Each individual enters new territory, and starts to discover new aspects of themselves that were not known before. All of this flows from you and your attitudes, responses, patience and kindness. As the teacher you are creating an atmosphere of respect, truth, and unlimited acceptance. You are creating a microcosm of how life can be when we truly honor each other.

As a result, the class feels safe to develop its own voice, its own wisdom, its own soul. It is a sort of oversoul that is supported by the soul of each individual student. Anything is possible. This collective heart of the class is, in many ways, the true teacher.

When questions arise, there is a quiet expectation that an answer will emerge from someone in the class, from you, or from the center of this learning community. There is an unspoken agreement that the

The soul is the perceiver and revealer of truth. We know the truth when we see it, let skeptic and scoffer say what they choose.

RALPH
WALDO
EMERSON

You cannot teach a man anything. You can only help him find it within himself.

GALILEO

wisdom of this community can solve just about anything. The class develops confidence in letting the process of each person, and that of the group, unfold in its own time.

Just as important as trusting the student is to trust the heart of the class. Unless you have had the experience of this first hand and have witnessed its power, it is hard to put into words this amazing dynamic. The class itself becomes a container to hold all the wisdom necessary to answer the questions of the students. Just by being in the class together, a dynamic develops that enables both students and teachers to learn more and understand more than any one individual could do alone.

This is the secret at the center of the class, referred to in the wonderful Robert Frost poem that says

"We dance around in a ring and suppose
but the Secret sits in the middle and knows."

THE LIFE OF THE CLASS

Each class takes on its own life besides any intention or outline that you may have set for it. Sometimes this is completely outside of the class topic. You may, for example, find that there is an ongoing discussion of romantic relationship because of the personal interests of the students, despite what the class topic is. Without any planning, you find yourself weaving relationship examples to make your discussions relevant. Perhaps there are worries over illness and again you find that the class discussion changes to include these concerns. The possibilities of this are endless. It is the mark of an excellent teacher when you can flex and flow with their interests.

Adults bring their entire life experience to their studies, and this will powerfully affect your class. Adult students have a deep desire to contribute, to be respected for their accomplishments and to find a sense of community with other adult learners. As you allow this richness to unfold, the class content and learning experience is transformed.

Additionally, you may find that the class conversation is constantly deepening on its own. I have learned to trust this process and to relate to it as the "secret at the center." Often, when the class takes an unexpected turn, you can depend on this secret wisdom to emerge. I have learned to put down my book or papers and wait, as we move into silence, and new wisdom will come forward from the group. Students will begin to share brilliant ideas and stories that are exactly what is needed at the time. It is not necessary for me to say a thing, but only to trust in the process of heart-based learning.

Recently, when teaching a class on Ethics, we were discussing how the challenges of life can sometimes be the greatest sources of understanding. One bright student offered:" Well, even war is a path to peace." The wisdom of this statement brought our discussions to a halt as everyone stopped to absorb the depth of its meaning. Many sessions later, other students would remind me of this statement and the impact it had on them. I loved this experience because when it happened, even the student who said it seemed surprised. A richer understanding had emerged than he could have found on his own.

It is impossible for you to manage this process other than to recognize its presence and let it take place. At most, you can bring your attention to your center, shore up your patience, and peacefully wait. The heart center of the class is calling forth a collective wisdom. I encourage you to trust this process.

Through learning we re-create ourselves. Through learning we become able to do something we were never able to do before.

PETER SENGE

TEACH WHO YOU ARE

In the challenging work of teaching adults, especially in topics of self-development, you must actively nurture your own perspectives of life. By this, I do not refer to any particular religion or philosophy. Instead, I mean your personal clarity about your own ethics, values, beliefs, and personal cosmology.

Take time for yourself to read and contemplate the larger issues of life. Spend some time each day in silence, quieting your mind, and listening to your heart. It is not possible to teach these kinds of classes without the smart adult student seeing exactly who you are. It was William Wordsworth who said:

> *"I see so clearly who you are that*
> *I cannot hear what you are saying."*

This is true of your students. They see you. You do not teach what you say, you teach who you are. It takes great courage to be a teacher today. In a public way, in the adult classroom, you asked to explore your own ignorance, as well as your own wisdom, and to be comfortable letting go of the control of the class so that your students may learn. Teaching is not a popularity contest. It is your powerful opportunity to make a true difference in our world by empowering your students, one by one.

The excellent teacher makes full use of their talents to create the best possible learning experience for their students. It requires a strong personal conviction that you are called to this important work, that these students are here on purpose, and that you respect them enough to teach them well.

To be nobody but myself in a world that is doing it's best, night and day,
to make you everybody else - means to fight the hardest battle
any human can fight and never stop fighting.
e e cummings

GROUNDED IN TRUTH

Set the intention that your classes will be solidly grounded in truth. Our world has had enough of lies and deceit in all arenas. In education, any sort of falsehood is a waste of everyone's time. Create your class as a safe space where anyone can speak a true statement about themselves, their lives, their reactions, their feelings. This is not license for anyone to insult, criticize or complain about anyone else. It is an opportunity for your students to learn to take responsibility for their feelings and attitudes, if they have not already done so.

Announce the basic rule: Everyone can speak for themselves on any topic as long as they use the word "I" and not the word "you" when expressing an opinion. Also train your students not to criticize each others statements, not to try to explain for each other, give a better example, or tell a better story.

Everyone must honor and respect each other enough to listen politely and accept what is said without argument. Everyone will get a chance to speak. With these rules, students can relax and be themselves. Maybe for the first time in their lives.

DOUBT AND CONFUSION

What shall we do when doubt and confusion arise in the classroom? This is not uncommon. Most important is to hear it out. This class must be a place where students can air their doubts. It is OK to hear the doubts and tough questions.

The doubting student is probably voicing the unspoken doubt of others. Just because someone is quiet does not mean that they are not in agreement with those voicing doubts. Open up and be willing to let these kinds of conversations take place in class. You do not have to have all the answers. Trust the process.

As these doubts emerge, wait until they begin to lose energy. Do not offer yourself as one who has all the answers. Rather wait and let the questions evolve in the room. Watch and see if the conversation can work itself out.

On the other hand, do not allow one doubt to build on another. Sometimes, in compassion, students begin to toss in their own fears, for the sake of compatibility. This situation is not good for the learning community. Just because we have created an honest space for each other does not mean that we are going to drag the conversation down to the lowest common denominator.

When things start to disintegrate into negativity, ask the positive question. Choosing your question can take practice. For example, let's say that the topic is our national economy. One student begins to share all of his doubts about whether the economic issues of our nation will ever run right. He begins to give examples of where things are going wrong. Other students begin to share their doubts, and fears begin to multiply on this subject. The discussion becomes heated. At what point will you intercede? Now is an important time to touch in with your inner teacher, the part of you that knows well how to teach this class. Consider: our purpose here is not to squelch the voicing of doubt and fear. Our purpose is to maintain an atmosphere of loving encouragement for all students.

So, when you feel the time is right, ask the positive question. "Do you have examples of where things *do* seem to be working?" or "Who can give an example of how this might change to work out better?" As students begin to consider the possibilities of a better way, they will begin to find new solutions, not only on this topic but for their personal lives.

The education of the heart cannot be imparted through books;
it can only be imparted through the loving work of the teacher.
CESAR CHAVEZ

At the same time, confusion is not yours to solve. In our American educational system, we often rush to clear away the student's confusion and try to explain it better or give the answers too soon. Especially in the work of personal growth and development, it is more empowering to allow the student to find their own way, if you can. Telling someone the answer is a weak substitute for letting the student find it for themselves.

This, again, is where experiential exercises come in. All the explanation in the world cannot replace five minutes of personal experience. When presenting difficult topics in class. plan time for an experiential exercise that will drive home the answer.

How you handle doubt and confusion in your classroom will be a barometer of how good of a teacher you truly are. Remember the secret in the center. The deep wisdom of the class is always emerging. Your role is to hold your own certainty that the answer is coming forward, and that each student has the native intelligence to find it for themselves.

Wisdom begins in wonder.

SOCRATES

THE SECRET OF SOCRATES

The great sage of ancient Greece, Socrates, famously used the idea of the "Secret at the Center" of the class and of the student. His idea was that the teacher was not responsible for pouring new information and ideas into the heads of ignorant students, but rather to draw out the native genius of each. He believed that universal truth lay below the surface of each conscious mind and could be drawn out by a skillful teacher. The art of teaching was just to ask a question. The student would find the truth within.

Socrates did not intend to expose what the student did not know, but rather to empower each student. Even the student did not, at first, understand his methods. But, his questions produced the realization that each held the truth within themselves. Each could count on themselves to find the answers and a personal truth they could never lose.

These are exciting ideas for the classroom. To use this method, you must be alert, patient, without ego and approach the student with love and good humor. It strips you of authority and places it in the hands of the student in a deeply validating way. It creates an ambiance in the classroom where anything is possible and the process of learning ignites into a blaze of truth.

I encourage you to follow the great Socrates and use the simple tools of query, love, respect and positive expectation to draw out the lesson from the lips of your students. Let your classroom foment with the give-and-take of question and answer. Speak to the center of your class and the genius of your students, as they find the answers within themselves. The results will dazzle you. The "secret at the center" will speak, students will transform before your eyes, and you will be grateful that by some good fortune of this life, you have been called to teach.

OPENING YOUR HEART

It is not possible to say enough about the importance of opening your heart to your great work of teaching. Love is the engine that drives the excellent teacher, and it is the yeast that causes mediocre classes to rise to unprecedented heights.

Love asks that you ignite in your students a passion for learning. Your fascination with your subject matter is contagious. Your joy and love of teaching create an atmosphere of personal expansion and growth for your adult student. The "secret at the center" of the class is not love, but the secret will dramatically flow through the class when love is present.

8. Special Issues with Students

HOW TO HANDLE CHALLENGING PEOPLE

In one of the first classes I ever taught, I had two challenging students. One was a highly respected professor from a nearby university, and the other was a local medical doctor. Both were taking night classes for their enrichment, and both felt that they had a lot to say - especially to each other. From the time these two men met, they conducted a constant verbal contest to out do each other.

They especially intended to out-talk me, as I was young and new at the game. It was the classic case of two experts in the classroom who think they should be the teacher, not the student. Much to the dismay of the other students. And to me, of course.

With my inexperience, I first began to engage with them, but almost immediately, I found this to be fruitless. I tried turning the discussion to other participants - also fruitless. I have since learned that it is possible to use your body, to stand right next to the expert student, and this will often quiet them down.

I learned quickly to not resist them and to wait them out. With no discussion, no response, no engagement from the rest of us, they eventually ran out of gas and came to a stop. At that point, I picked up the thread of the class with some new material outside of their experience level and regained control of the discussion.

It is important that students bring a certain ragamuffin barefoot irreverence to their studies; they are not here to worship what is known, but to question it.

JACOB BRONOWSKI

Having this experience so early on, I have learned to not fear these challenging situations and neither should you. The adult wants respect in the classroom, and if they do not get it, they will demand it from you. Other students will often join forces with anyone who they feel you are slighting in the classroom. So, even challenging students must have your respect and attention.

It is part of the fun of teaching adults. You have the opportunity to engage with these students as equals and still manage to teach them something new. This is challenging, important work. It is constantly surprising. In every session, there are special circumstances that create an opportunity for you to expand in your skill. This chapter will deal with a few of these special issues.

FEAR

In every adult class, the teacher must be prepared to address issues of fear. Our culture does not often provide many opportunities, such as your classroom, where individuals can share and discuss their innermost ideas, feelings and experiences. We have devoted much attention here to creating your class as a safe space for these personal revelations to take place. However, you must still be ready to counter the deep-seated fears many have of participating in this way.

One approach is to be very aware of the configurations of your exercises. Many who will not reveal themselves in large groups will do so in one-on-one experiences. Male students may be comfortable speaking only with women or perhaps only with men. With sensitive topics, students may only touch in deeply when they are journaling or doing other writing that no one else will see. The

Before my education began, I was without compass or sounding line, no way of knowing how near the harbor was. "Light! Give me light! was the wordless cry of my soul, and the light of love shown on me in that very hour.
HELEN KELLER

basic tenant of this topic is that fear is present only because the individual is not feeling secure enough to let their true feelings or ideas be known. There is nothing wrong with this in any way. But, as the instructor, you know that the stronger posture for the student is to be comfortable with their truth. To let themselves be known. Your task is to midwife this idea into your class.

It goes, perhaps without saying, that ANY revelation must be greatly welcomed and appreciated. No matter what anyone shares in your class, it must be safe to do so. I often like to remind my students of the power of just saying their truth or new ideas out loud. By speaking it aloud, it becomes more dynamic and real. Explaining this idea clearly will often encourage your students to speak.

It is a careful process, and I encourage you in being patient about it. Over time, your students will come to trust your kindness. They may even let go of old fearful ideas and speak out. In extreme cases, when you see someone imprisoned by fear, you may wish to meet outside of class with her and see if you can support her in releasing these old fears. Life is short and much too brief for us to remain imprisoned inside, unable to share fully who we are.

That is the difference between good teachers and great teachers. Good teachers make the best of a pupil's means; great teachers forsee a pupil's ends.

MARIA CALLAS

FEARLESSNESS

On the other side of this discussion is the student who is fearless. This, surprisingly, can be equally challenging in class. The fearless one may wear many guises. He may be one who is always ready to monopolize the class having his own powerful experience of his own truth. She can be one who moves ahead faster than anyone else and moves into new topics or risks new behaviors before the class groundwork has been laid. In worst cases, he may be one who feels just fine about speaking his opinion of you, the class, the process and the other students. She may even lean into the idea of taking over the teaching of the class and present a challenge to you in that way.

In taming the fearless student, it is important to remember that you are the teacher. Regardless of the experience level of the student vs yourself, or of your kind heart which wants to support this student, or any other reason you can conjure up, you are still the teacher. You are called to this work. We know this simply because you are sitting in the teacher's seat. So, yours is the long view of this situation. Our goal is to empower this student and still encourage balance.

So, let us take this one case at a time.

If your student is fearless about his own processes and monopolizes your class discussions, you must rein him in. It can be as simple as asking "Who else has something to contribute?" Or, you may choose this student to use as an example, carefully sifting through his comments and using it as a test case to show your course content is at work in his life. If neither of these approaches

CHARACTERS IN YOUR CLASSROOM

DOC: The Expert. A potential group leader. Knows it all. Can challenge you or the other students. Give him some air time and move on.

HAPPY: Excited, upbeat, loves to reinforce you positively. Is he real?

BASHFUL: Shy, introverted. Often very smart. Give her some safe tasks to do: closing doors, passing out papers. Draw out gently. Talk privately. Don't insist on sharing.

SNEEZY: Reactive, always sick, out of touch with his body and feelings. Has coughing fits or often feels ill in class. Misses class. Her body is talking to her. What is it saying?

SLEEPY: Too stressed or emotional to participate. May even fall sleep during class. Don't worry. As long as she continues to show up, she is learning something.

GRUMPY: The critic. Never satisfied. Sees the flaw in everything (especially in himself). He is your guardian of truth. Make him an ally, and he is yours forever.

DOPEY: Just doesn't get it. Blocked. Avoid giving him a monopoly on your time. Discourage the class from adopting him as their pet project. Relax. He will find his way in his own time.

seems workable, you might consider offering him the opportunity to journal his experiences privately to you. Remember to encourage this student in every way, except in monopolizing the class.

If she is one who moves ahead faster and risks new behaviors before you have laid the necessary groundwork, she must be stopped. This is a sensitive area because, by definition, the adult learner adores freedom and independence in pursuing their experience.

So, unfortunately, it is necessary to remind this fearless student of what she does not know. You can choose to be patient about this or not, depending on the situation. The underlying idea here is that you are responsible for seeing that this student has the proper preparation and information.

The most direct approach is just to ask her. You can do this privately or in class. A simple question will do: "Did you consider the research on this when you.....?" Or, how did you approach this given the reading in......?" Refer to material that the class did not cover, and the student does not know.

Her attempts to answer your question will prove your point. Once you can point out areas she does not know, it is important to be supportive and encouraging in her keeping pace with the class. This is a subtle approach.

If this subtle kind of questioning does not work, you may consider meeting with her privately and slowing her down. Let her know that the class dynamic will support her in being the leader she obviously is. By keeping pace with the class, she can reinforce and deepen her understanding of the topic as well as visit new perspectives offered by the other students. Is she listening to them?

In other type of fearlessness, the student feels free to criticize

Education is the ability to listen to almost anything without losing your temper or your self-confidence.

ROBERT FROST

*They
are able
who
think
they are
able.*

VIRGIL

others and potentially challenge your leadership of the class. It may be due to fearlessness, ignorance or the inexperience of the student.

No matter what the cause, you must take action on this one. The wisest approach is always to do this privately, meeting with the student and telling him that it is not part of our class to criticize each other. This is a safe space for everyone. If, after this meeting, the behavior continues, you may need to ask him to leave the class.

You can also consider handling this within the class itself. To do this, you must be prepared to explain that we do not criticize each other and to counter any debate that may follow. This approach is highly effective many times in stopping the behavior. However, it can antagonize the class to see you pick on one of its own. Even if the other students completely understand that the behavior is inappropriate, they will almost always object to your confronting the student in class. So, I am not saying never to do this, but rather to be very careful to speak lovingly and with respect for the student involved. In rare cases, the rest of the students will solve this kind of problem themselves through class interactions. But don't count on it.

QUESTIONS OF AGE

What is there to say about age in the classroom? Well, if you are a young teacher there is a lot to be aware of when your students are substantially older. If you are a lot older than your students, age will also play a factor. Here are a few ideas about issues of age.

Do not debate a student whose age is different from yours if they raise age-related issues. For example, if you are very young and your student is worried about retirement, treat this issue with respect and do not pretend to know how they might feel. Or if you are quite a bit older and your student is discussing problems in life that you have already solved, do not give advice. Listen with respect and do not tread into areas where you are not wanted.

Try to keep abreast of issues and interests of all age groups. Teaching adults is an excellent motivation to subscribe to diverse magazines, watch a wide spectrum of movies, visit a wide array of stores, read a variety of newspapers, stay up to date online. Become a student of our culture and all of the issues facing every age today.

Wait for the wisest of all counselors - time.

PERICLES

CREDIBILITY ISSUES

By definition, you have credibility as the teacher. Credibility is yours to lose in the classroom. You may have someone in the class who is smarter, more experienced, and has more force of personality than you do. It has nothing to do with credibility. You are not teaching because you are stronger, braver, smarter, more experienced, or more attractive. You are teaching because you have a passion and a calling to teach.

So, what to do about challenging students? Nothing. Place your feet firmly on the ground and do not concern yourself with their challenges. If they have more experience, create a welcoming space for them to share and receive the praise of their peers.

If they ask questions you cannot answer, say simply "I don't know. Let's discuss this with the class and see what they think." If they share their opinions forcefully, stay cool and calm. Ask for other opinions. Relax. The way to maintain credibility is to be sure in your own mind that you are in charge. Open the discussion and enjoy it.

RELATIONSHIPS WITH THE STUDENTS

You must find your own level of relating to your students. It is easy to be very friendly and sociable with them. The class appreciates your friendliness and openness. However, you cross the line when you socialize with your students outside of class. Once you develop a personal relationship with your students, you enter new territory that can undermine your efforts to teach them. I believe it goes without saying that never should you date one of your students. All professionals who do inner work know this. But romantic relationships aside, it is compromising to develop personal relationships with your students while you have them in class.

Just by definition, friendships create a level of intimacy that will undermine your authority and power as a teacher. Take yourself seriously as a teacher and keep a high professional standard. If you find yourself wanting to socialize with your students, ask yourself: Am I giving my social nature enough attention? Create ways of making new friends on your own time and expand your social activities. Set a goal to have more fun and live a more balanced life

Later, when the class is over, if you want to socialize with someone you met in class, it is up to you. After the class is over, you are free to create any level of relationship you choose to have, knowing that you have given your best as a teacher and now you can give your best as a friend.

You suppose you are the trouble, But you are the cure.
You suppose you are the lock on the door, But you are the key that opens it.
It's too bad you want to be someone else.
You don't see your own face, your own beauty,
Yet, no face is more beautiful than yours.
RUMI

9. Closings

POWERFUL WAYS TO COMPLETE YOUR SESSIONS

The human heart is not willing to invest time and energy into a class and have it stop suddenly, with no importance given to its ending. Just as the openings of classes are important, so are the closings. It is true of each individual class session and the course as a whole. Do your students a great favor by giving thoughtful consideration to how the class will end. Here are a few ideas to consider.

A teacher affects eternity. He can never tell where his influence stops.

HENRY ADAMS

SUMMARIES

Doing a summary for adult learners is a big winner. It can work at every session and succeeds powerfully at the end of the course. The adult learner likes to be reminded of what they have accomplished.

1. I have not wasted my time - Summary

In your summary, stress the importance of the application of your subject to the students' personal and professional lives. It speaks well of your busy students that they have taken the time and effort to go back to school. They are motivated, sincere in their interest, willing to learn and grow. Address this directly in your summary and affirm that they have spent their precious time well.

2. I learned a lot - Summary

Recap the entire class from the beginning, and remind the students of

Keep away from those who belittle your ambitions. The really great make you feel that you, too, can become great.

MARK TWAIN

all the has been covered, and the conclusions that have been reached. This may be very apparent to you, but the student has a busy mind and will deeply appreciate your summarizing the journey for them.

3. I feel I played an important part in the class - Summary

Congratulate the class on how well they did the work. Give a few special thank you's to those who participated strongly, and remind the class of how much we all enjoyed being together. It may sound a little overdone, but I suggest you try it and see the collective pleasure such a summary will invoke in the class.

4. I have an opinion about this experience - Summary

Go around the class and ask each person to speak a word or two of what they received from the class, or what their favorite moment was, or how they are feeling about the material now. Adults love to be asked for their opinion. This can be a satisfying end to the class.

Ideas for Closing Rituals

- Ask each student to say what they are taking away from this class.
- Go around the room and honor each student. Give each student a chance to publicly thank each of the others for their contribution to the class.
- Ask each student to light a candle of their intention for the future. As they do this, the class affirms agreement with them.
- Post a long piece of paper on the wall and give out markers. Ask each to draw what the class meant to them in one long mural. Take a class picture with their masterpiece. Give everyone a copy of the photo.
- Bring each student to the front of the class or center of the circle and present them with a certificate of completion. Let them say a few words.
- A closing party or feast to celebrate as a joyous ritual for a job well done.

FINAL PROJECTS AND PRESENTATIONS

Final projects can lend a great deal of power to the student's learning experience. The entire last session devoted to the presentation of the final projects can serve as a satisfying way to close the class. Students are often impressed to see their fellow student's work, and the impact of this can make a lasting impression.

Final projects also give each student an opportunity to summarize their class experience in a way that is not only memorable, but serves to drive home the importance of the class material in a very personal way.

For all of these reasons, you are making a significant choice when assigning the final project for your class. It is important, I believe, to not expect the student to regurgitate your class material or to present a research paper of someone else's view on the subject. Rather, consider how the student can integrate the class substance into their personal experience of their life. How will this material be used to make the individual's life better?

Consider an abstract portrayal of a concrete subject. Or a concrete presentation of an abstract subject. For example, if you have been studying someone's written work, how would the student picture this information being used in the world?

Visual presentation demands that the student grasp the import of the written word and its logical results. The student might use photographs, drawings, collage or other visual tools to portray this result. This presentation will spark discussion in the class.

Conversely, ask the student to write a poem or a story that represents an abstract idea such as a math concept, a painting or other ideas you have been working with in class. In this case, the the student takes an abstract idea and brings it down to earth. Once again, good grist for class discussion.

*He who
knows
others is
learned;
he who
knows
himself
is wise.*

LAO TZE

Consider a very personal final project. The student can answer the question: "How has my life changed because of this class?" The project can be anything that symbolizes this change.

Sometimes it is fun for the class to do a final project in teams. If this is a good idea for your class, be sure that each team member participates. Create a simple check-off sheet for each student to grade each of their teammates in participation and creativity and helpfulness. If the final project is a team project, encourage creativity. Suggest ideas such as staging a debate, a short skit, or an interactive exercise for the class.

A powerful idea is to ask each student to prepare a final project that represents what they have learned. In every case, the project should be the capstone for the class. Through discussion of these projects, the student body will more clearly grasping the overall concepts of the class.

Encourage students in being imaginative and personal in their projects. If appropriate, invite their families to this final day. Celebrate each student and each project. The work has been completed, and you have shared a significant experience as a class. Celebrate and honor everyone involved.

LETTING GO

An important part of ending your class is to do the personal work to separate yourself from this group and the work that has been accomplished. Do this in your private time, when the assignments are complete, and the sessions are over. As a teacher, you give so much of yourself and now is the time to take care of you.

Create a space of stillness. Reflect upon the class, all that happened, the parts you liked and parts you did not like. What will you improve next time? Contemplate your students and all that they gave to you and all you gave to them.

Give yourself the chance to grow from this experience. How is your heart more open because of this class? What do you know now that you did not know before the class began? What do you understand more deeply about your life and about your way of teaching? Journal about these things. Allow yourself time to sit still. Let your thoughts and feelings flow. And then let it go.

You may wish to visualize collecting up the class as a ball of energy and tossing it back to the students for their future. You may wish to take a hot shower and imagine the water washing the class from your body and your life.

You may wish to do your own ritual of completion by writing down all the things about the class to release and then burning the paper. Or blowing out a candle. You may wish to make a threshold of the classroom exit and step over it, turning off the light, leaving the class behind.

Whatever you choose to do, take the time to arrive at personal completion of the class by letting it all go. Doing this restores your energy, frees up your mind, expands your heart and opens up the future for the great work you will do next.

The best thing for being sad, replied Merlyn.." is to learn something. That is the only thing that never fails. You may grow old and trembling in our anatomies, you may lie awake at night listening to the disorder of your veins,...you may see the world around you devastated by evil lunatics, or know your honor trampled in the sewers of baser minds. There is only one thing for it then - to learn. Learn why the world wags and what wags it. That is the only thing which the mind can never exhaust, never alienage, never be tortured by, never fear or distrust, and never dream of regretting. Learning is the thing for you.

T.H.WHITE, The Once and Future King

10. The Inner Life of Teaching

KEEPING AN OPEN HEART EVERY DAY

The great work of being a teacher is not one that many undertake. It is an inspired, essentially selfless role to be the one who guides others into their personal empowerment and new levels of expertise. Every day puts new demands on the teacher: demands of extra patience, thoroughness, expanding creativity, and creating new ways for inspiring others.

Besides the noble art of getting things done, there is the noble art of leaving things undone.

HELENA BLAVATSKY

Most importantly, it demands that the teacher find a way to keep an open heart every day, to be available to students with a constant stream of imagination, that is so essential to doing this work. In this chapter, we will discuss these demands of the inner life and how to keep the flame of love for this work burning in your heart.

DAILY CARE

As each day provides a new beginning, it also provides an opportunity to fine-tune your daily schedule into one that nourishes your body, mind and spirit. Starting with the first light of day, take time for yourself. Greet the sun with some moments of personal silence and contemplation. Let go of all the detail of life and open up your mind to peace. Play some soft music if you like, or pour a hot cup of tea. Connect with your inner teacher. Ask yourself, "What am I to know today? What am I giving to life and what am I receiving?" Listen for the answers in your heart. Sit in the still of the morning and let your heart be steeped in the flow of inner knowing. Open your heart and send love out to your students. Open your heart to yourself, and appreciate who you are and all that you do.

Let your early morning be as a sacrament in your life. Prepare a nourishing breakfast. Eat it carefully, and be glad for your health. Do some exercise to get your body started - whatever form you choose. It is wonderful to make a ritual of a morning outdoor walk: good for the body and good for the soul. Be present to the beauty of nature around you.

Choose clothing that is comfortable and encouraging to you. Take the time to care for it well, and feel your best as you wear it. Care for your home and take a few moments each morning to tidy up a bit, hang things up, and make it a welcoming place to come home to after class.

Take time during the day to find a few quiet moments. Refresh, replenish, restore yourself. Teaching demands a full reservoir of energy, ideas, enthusiasm and inspiration. Give yourself time each day to fill back up. At the end of the day, celebrate your life. Have some fun, relax. Make a list of all you love about this day. Get a good restful sleep and know that your time today was well spent.

Writing Pages in the Morning

Julia Cameron, author of <u>The Artist's Way</u>, created this way of letting your mind unwind itself first thing in the morning by writing anything and everything that comes into your head. There is no sense to this, except it works. Start with a fresh sheet of paper each morning and let your stream of consciousness flow. Write all the negative things you can think of, all the positive things and anything else that comes up. The task is to download everything that is occupying your thinking. Spend at least 15 minutes with this exercise each morning. After a few weeks, note the positive results of clarity, contentment, and focus that result.

WALLOWING IN BEAUTY

Where do you find your inspiration to teach? In your private moments, it is powerful to consider the inner well that sources your creative teaching ideas, your patience for your students, your passion for your subject matter, your willingness to be a mentor for others.

The demands of your work are tremendous. You cannot expect to continue class after class with this profound level of giving yourself without finding equally powerful ways of filling back up. Exercise will help, as will good rest, nutritious food, fun with friends. I encourage you to all of these.

Yet, the great restorer of your soul is beauty. Beauty is that quality of life that cannot be put into words. Everyone has their own idea of what it truly is. By spending time with beauty, by gazing upon it, listening to its melody, feeling it in your heart, you will again find your balance. Beauty reminds us of the wonder of life that is always present, but so often we are too busy to pay attention to it.

To enrich your life, set an intention to spend time with beauty every day. Wallow in it. Revel in it. Let it speak its wordless message to your soul. Let it take root in your heart and fill you with awe and gratitude. Embrace the abundant beauty of life in all of its glory.

In my own worst seasons I've come back from the colorless world of despair
by forcing myself to look hard, for a long time, at a single glorious thing:
a flame of red geranium outside my bedroom window. And then another:
my daughter in a yellow dress. And another: the perfect outline of a full, dark
sphere behind the crescent moon. Until I learned to be in love with my life again.
Like a stroke victim retraining new parts of the brain to grasp lost skills,
I have taught myself joy, over and over again.

BARBARA KINGSOLVER
High Tide in Tucson: Essays from Now or Never

Here are a few suggestions for adding daily beauty to your life.

- Walk outside and think of nothing but the natural beauty you see.

- Add music to your home. Sit and listen to a favorite song all the way through.

- Consider the colors of your home and clothing. Play with color.

- Add a pretty plant or fresh flowers to your desk.

- Spend time in a local art gallery and soak in the paintings' beauty.

- Pour water in a colored dish and watch the reflections in the sun

- Pay attention at sunrise and sunset.

- Keep track of the moon. Experiment with a moonlight meditation.

- Hike. Play a sport. Dance to music and feel your body rejoice.

SUSTAINING YOUR CREATIVITY

Creativity, like every other aspect of our personality, suffers from long hours, not enough rest, and too much routine pressure. Almost by definition, creativity demands fresh, free, delicious time in which you can let go of the need to create and turn your attention to something else.

When you feel emotionally drained, even sleep will not restore you. By focusing your attention on something else, you begin to use lateral thinking that brings unexpected solutions and ideas to you. How to sustain your creativity? By taking the time off to do something else.

Before we go further with this topic, however, let's be clear that vegging in front of the TV does not help. It does perhaps rest your poor tired head, but it does not help your creativity. To recharge and sustain a high-level flow of creative ideas, you must get into motion.

Creativity is like a willful child that will not come when it is called. You must entice it back home, when it has gone astray or just refuses to play. A foolproof way is to begin to create something new that has absolutely no purpose in the world to anyone other than you.

This might be taking up new craft or something that you can do with your hands: carpentry, painting, sewing, gardening - anything with your hands. At the very least, get yourself some crayons or colored pens and set aside a time to doodle or color every day. Allowing creativity to come out in new, lighthearted ways is enormously refreshing. It is a fun addition to your life.

Any task that improves your daily life will also start to recharge you. OK, clean the garage or the closets. Sort out that messy drawer. Wash the car. Polish the furniture. Do something that absorbs your attention and rests your mind. Do a crossword puzzle, a jigsaw puzzle or sudoku. Put on some music and dance until you are tired. Read some poetry. Take a long walk in nature.

As you turn your attention to these restful pastimes, your creativity starts to return. Don't forget the tonic of a good laugh. Go to a funny movie or comedy club. Go out with friends and laugh. Enjoy the satisfying pleasures of the body: a hot bath, great massage, time for love. A great or even profound stress relief.

As you do these things, forget your daily grind and just let your mind rest. Realize that life is not so serious that you cannot enjoy these simple pleasures. Gradually, you will find new ideas appearing and your zest for life returning. Your deep inner well of creativity is filling up again.

Learning is finding out what we already know.
Doing is demonstrating that we know it.
Teaching is reminding others that they know
just as well as you.
We are all learners, doers and teachers.

RICHARD BACH

THE IMPORTANCE OF A SUPPORT NETWORK

You have been called to teach. Yours is somewhat solitary path of leadership and vision. It need not be a lonely path, if you develop an important support network. If you are to be a source of inspiration, growth and ideas for others, you must offer these gifts from a full life experience of your own. You cannot look to your work as a place where you can relax and reveal your personal self. Your work cannot share your personal dreams. It cannot tell you when to take a vacation. It certainly cannot help you develop your goals for the future. Your support network is the place for all of this and more. A place where you can blow off steam, laugh over mistakes and lay down the mantle of teacher for a while.

Who will it be? Who will you turn to for support? Spouses, family and close friends come to mind first as likely prospects. This may not be true. Remember that your intimate relationships hold a unique place in your life, and you need them to be separate from your work life. These are the closest people in your life who know all sides of you, and travel the path of life with you in important ways. They support you by just being there. They will be there if you quit working, change your work or retire. You experience love, joy and personal sharing with them. They fill an important role in your life, and they are not the best ones for your professional support network.

Rather look for people that are like you: teachers or those doing similar work. Those who share your professional standards and are excited about what they do. Those who have many ideas and have positive input on your day-to-day issues, questions, challenges and opportunities as a teacher. People you can talk with, laugh with, and turn to when you are discouraged with your work.

You will find them where you teach, at conferences, professional development classes, possibly online. Start with one and try to find four or five; individuals you can call, have coffee with, share ideas with, and lean on to inspire you. As you take care of yourself this way, you come to your day refreshed and ready to do your best work.

WHAT TO DO WITH YOUR CERTAINTY

Being a teacher is a strange business. On one hand, you spend years digging deeply into your subjects, mastering your topics, perfecting your skills, and doing all that you can to be of service to your students. As the years go by, you develop pride in your work and feel capable of handling the challenges of the day. This is a great accomplishment and marks you as good at what you do.

Certainty can, however, carry a dark shadow of rigidity with it. Not all at once. No. It creeps up slowly when you get too busy, take on too much, don't take time for yourself, forget to call someone from your support team. All of a sudden you find yourself saying the same thing over and over. You decide you don't have to do the class reading, since you already know it.

You find yourself impatient with student questions and having the weird feeling that not only do you know all the answers, you also know all the questions. Your classes become predictable and more narrow, easily repeatable and even forgettable. Most importantly, you lose your interest in other approaches, or off the wall ideas that may pop up in the class discussions.

This is really boredom masquerading as certainty. You must do something about it. If you were teaching children, it would be wise to stop teaching at the current level and take on a new challenge. Fortunately, you are teaching adults, and you have other choices. This is an opportunity to let your students to shine.

The new choice is to redo your class so that your adult students can do most of the work. Oh yes. This is an excellent choice and moves you in the direction of

---

As I teach,
I project the condition of my soul
onto my students, my subject, and our way of being together.

PARKER PALMER

greater excellence. It will give you a badly needed break and give your students a chance to participate. It will open up the attic of your mind to a be ways of teaching. Your old certainty will melt away and in its place will be the fresh new excitement of what is possible.

Spend a weekend going back over your materials and reorganizing so that the students can take over parts of the class. Go through the suggestions of this book and form panels, interview teams, research projects, discussion groups, games, and stories for your students. Let the class decide on its own goals and direction. Take on a new persona and simply serve as a resource for them.

It will feel like a vacation for you, and your students will grow and lead, right before your eyes. Relax. Sit back and enjoy your latest creation: the participative learning experience. Go home and read a good book, take up hiking or play tennis, and let your students carry the load for a while. Buy a new notebook to record all the great ideas you are learning from them. Until you feel ready and recharged enough to start again. Or, who knows? You may find this grand experiment so enjoyable that you never go all the way back to carrying the load of knowledge for everyone else. This is the heart of adult education. We grow and experience together. The more involved your students are, the more they will shine. And the more they will love their learning experience with you.

SELF-CONTROL

I would like to say a word here about the wildly unpopular idea of self-control. Even the words themselves sound like a morals tale from our childhood. This is an important idea to consider in the deep inner realms of your life. The question becomes: what are you teaching yourself through all of this? Life is short, and all we have is the precious time of our days to spend. Are you spending yours in ways that nourish you and allow you to grow? Consider the patterns you are living.

It's so easy when tired or overworked to indulge yourself. Maybe its vegging in front of the TV, eating the wrong foods, sleeping the wrong hours, forgetting to exercise. All easily understandable and explainable. If repeated over and over, these things lead to a life that is unhealthy, more stressful and unhappy.

So, take a few moments each morning, when doing your morning pages, and make a list of how you will deal today with your stresses and disappointments. Pay close attention. Discover that a long walk will relieve stress more than not moving. Regular sleep habits will bring more joy than overeating, over drinking or other excess. Call on your support group for a discussion over coffee, instead of watching TV. Say to yourself: "I am learning to manage my own happiness".

This is equally important with your thinking. Avoid negative friends and let them share their pessimism with someone else. Turn off the news. Spend time in nature. Make a list of those who frustrate you, annoy you, or disappoint you. Decide to try to love them, just for one day. Turn off violent TV and avoid dark movies. Think of your mind as a beautiful tool you use to help others to grow and learn. Refuse to pollute it with needless negativity. Decide to love yourself exactly as you are. Decide to manage this self, yourself, and live your best life.

If we value independence, if we are disturbed by the growing conformity of knowledge, of values, of attitudes, which our present system induces, then we may wish to set conditions of learning which make for uniqueness, for self-direction and for self-initiated learning.

CARL ROGERS

YOUR INNER WORLD

You are called to teach. What a wonderful thing. Do you realize how special you are? Aside from your paycheck, your living circumstances, your challenges, all the little details of life, you are a great person and hold a high position among us.

We look to you to guide us, support us, shine the light for us, lead us into new ways of understanding, new ways of living, new ways of being who we are. We look to you, depend upon you, admire you in more ways than you will ever know. You are more loved and appreciated than you can imagine.

As you walk through your days, let these ideas remind you of the great life you came here to live. You give so much. Give attention to yourself and your own heart. Create spaces of time when you are still. Find a quiet place, sit comfortably, close your eyes and let life wash over you. Become familiar with the sound of your own breath, the beating of your own heart. Draw deeply from the well of love that lives within you.

There are so many ways to do this. If you like music, find a special piece and simply sit, letting the music carry you. Try chanting or humming or rocking gently and rhythmically in place. Stretch out on the floor and float away.

Take your problems and questions into the silent center of your heart. Do this at a regular time each day. Ask for answers from a wisdom higher than your surface mind. Let your intuition have its voice and speak.

Just as there is a secret at the center of every class, there is a secret at the center of you. It is an inner genius, a boundless spirit, a flow of love, and the presence of greatness. Take yourself each day to this temple of your own truth. Grow your inner life. Within is the rich source of all the greatest ideas and wisdom you can depend on, as one who teaches through the heart.

Thank you for saying yes to the call to teach.

*Education is not the filling of a pail,
but the lighting of a fire.*

W.B.YEATS

If you are interested in emailing me
or in finding more resources for teaching,
please visit my website
www.theheartofteaching.com

Made in the USA
Charleston, SC
30 June 2016